Cuba

The Struggle for Consumption

Anna Cristina Pertierra

Cuba; The Struggle for Consumption.

Author: Anna Cristina Pertierra

Photos in Figures 1, 2 , 3, 4, 6, 7 and 8 reprinted with permission of: Gabrielle Hosein; All other photos, courtesy of the author.

Cover design: Cédric Sébastien Casséus

Library of Congress Control Number: 2011932382

For more information, please contact

Caribbean Studies Press.

7550 NW 47th Avenue,

Coconut Creek, FL 33073

Telephone: (954) 968-7433

E-mail: educa@aol.com

Web: www.educavision.com

ISBN: 978-1-58432-753-0

Table of Contents

Acknowledgments

In the years that have passed since I first began my research in Santiago de Cuba in 2003, my relationship with the city and with many of the people who appear in this book changed substantially. Far from being a mere "research site," professionally and personally my life has been tremendously enriched – if sometimes complicated – by having Santiago de Cuba become a part of it. My family has grown to incorporate not only a partner, but wonderful in-laws. My daughter Ana Maria, whose birth has connected me in yet deeper ways to Cuba, was christened in the church of the Virgen de la Caridad del Cobre. During this period, "my" Santiago de Cuba has grown to encompass Spain, Italy, the United States and of course Australia, where I have continued to keep up with friends first met during my research who have moved, just as my own family has become one far-flung part of the Cuban diaspora. I have been lucky enough to keep returning to Santiago de Cuba, and to the people in the Tivolí without whom my research would have been impossible. To preserve their privacy, I am unable to acknowledge those individuals by name. At the Universidad de Oriente, the early support of Graciela Durán, Teresa Reyes, Maricel Sansó and Jorge Ariosa was essential.

Many people have assisted me in the writing and editing of this manuscript: in London from 2003 to 2007, Daniel Miller always went well beyond the call of duty in reading my work. Martin Holbraad, Ruth Mandel, Nanneke Redclift, fellow members of the "dinner group" and others from my cohort at University College London also gave me important feedback for which I am thankful. Richard Wilk and Olivia

Harris have also been exceptionally generous supporters of my research and my career, and I am only sorry that the latter is not able to read this book herself. Since joining the University of Queensland in 2008, my colleagues at the Centre for Critical and Cultural Studies have patiently listened to later versions of this work, and the energy and support of Graeme Turner in helping me complete a piece of research that is really quite unrelated to his own interests has been especially important. Thanks also to Elizabeth Kath, Judith Pugh, Robert J. Foster, and the anonymous reviewers of an earlier version of this manuscript. At Caribbean Studies Press, it has been a true pleasure to work with Carol Hollander.

Several members of my family – Lyn Shoemark, Raul Pertierra, Karel Reyes, Margarita González-Rodiles and Edelmira "Nena" González – have enabled me to write this book with their various forms of support, whether through proofreading pages, listening to ideas, taking on childcare, freeing me from housework, or generally understanding my commitment to the project of research and writing. Ana Maria understands no such thing, and her total indifference to this book has allowed me to enjoy entirely different kinds of pleasure as her mother alongside the more arduous achievements that come from trying to be an anthropologist.

A Guide to Terminology

The retention of a dual economy in Cuba since 1993, and the various changes that have taken place within such a dual economy, have created an abundance of everyday terms that can be confusing to the reader. Three major currencies have been used in Cuba since the 1990s. Prices and payments quoted throughout this book adopt the most relevant currency for that particular transaction, and the currency in question is always identified using the terminology explained below:

Moneda nacional, abbreviated to MN or CUP, was the standard currency until the fall of the Soviet Union, and remains in use for many formal and informal transactions. In this book I adopt the English term "Cuban pesos." Generally, from 2000 to date, between 25 and 27 Cuban pesos has been equivalent to one US dollar.

The *peso Cubano convertible,* abbreviated to CUC, was introduced in 1993 at a rate fixed to the US dollar. It is used to pay for specific goods and services that have been introduced since 1993, including tourist-oriented services. In this book I use the English term "convertible pesos" along with the abbreviation CUC.

US dollars were legal tender in Cuba from 1993 until 2004, and until that time were used interchangeably with convertible pesos. Despite no longer using US dollars in Cuban stores, *dólares* or dollars are often mentioned in vernacular conversation referring, for example, to goods that must be bought in convertible pesos.

Introduction

Studying Scarcity in Post-Soviet Cuba

On the streets of the neighborhood known as El Tivolí, there is energy and excitement every day, and every day, nothing happens. People are bored, and therefore enter into every moment and transaction with gusto. There is dancing, laughing, yelling, gossiping, playing, loafing, staring and just passing time. Sitting on doorsteps, hair in rollers and small children within sight, young women in faded Lycra talk about their boyfriends' latest exploits. A little further inside the open front door, old women sit in their *balances* (rocking chairs), greeting neighbors and recounting conversations with other people. On the corner or in the square sit the men, grouped according to age, but all doing the same things; smoking, drinking rum, playing dominoes and arguing about sport. Schoolchildren – *pioneros*, "the pioneers" – immaculately turned out with their clean white shirts and their little red neckties, struggle along the street with their backpacks and small lunches in baskets and thermoses. Occasionally there is evidence of "work"; street vendors pushing noisy homemade carts, singing out their wares. Fumigators in grey overalls, spraying toxic-looking fumes from door to door in the public campaign against mosquitoes. Motorbike taxis, mostly driven by proud young men, charging 10 pesos a ride to those with means to avoid the crowded buses and long, hot walks; young women in heels and miniskirts deftly mounting the back of the bike and clutching the driver; middle-aged schoolteachers demurely sitting side-saddle and begging the driver not to speed; men carrying Technicolor cakes for a child's birthday party, and glamorous young men and women wearing brand-name clothing and big sunglasses, hunting foreigners and dollars.

Nobody runs, or even walks quickly; when possible, people don't move at all, instead they yell across spaces, or send a child to complete an errand. Nobody, and nothing, is quiet. The concept of tranquility, were it conceivable, would be unsettling, as to exist in the Tivolí is to make and to live amid noise. Below the sounds of vendors selling, fumigators fumigating, motorbikes revving, are televisions yelling, salsa music blaring, pigs squealing, children crying, visitors visiting, couples fighting, bands rehearsing, dominoes click-clacking and everybody always talking.

Within this vibrant environment I spent a little over a year conducting fieldwork in 2003 and 2004, attempting to understand the patterns, products and ideas that shape everyday life for urban citizens in post-Soviet Cuba. Subsequent follow-up visits in 2006, 2008 and 2009 allowed me to revisit many of my original informants in the

Tivolí, to keep up with their changing lives, while also undertaking wider research in other parts of Santiago de Cuba and expanding my study to consider new topics. Therefore, although a part of this study focuses on the Tivolí as a community with a distinct history and identity, in other ways the experiences and activities of its inhabitants are representative of the various challenges and opportunities found across most urban areas in contemporary Cuba. Residents I worked with were neither the richest nor the poorest Cubans around, were not unusually active or powerful in political and cultural circles but moderately engaged with civic and community events. They enjoyed housing conditions that were generally better than those in the poorest municipalities of southeastern Cuba, but which paled in comparison to the smartest apartments and houses of Havana, with reliable water supplies, satellite television and washing machines. Soon after arriving in Santiago de Cuba, I puzzled over what seemed to me to represent the beginning, if not the solution, to unpacking the complexities of daily life within this community: I was struck by the simultaneous sensation of people doing a great deal but achieving very little, which seemed not only to shape the patterns and rhythms of every life, but also lies at the heart of many joys as well as many frustrations that Cubans express about living in contemporary Cuba. The Tivolí is a hive of activity, within which much sociality, but not much else, seems to be achieved or produced. This is why travel journalists write about the ambience, the *mañana* mentality; stressed Europeans should take a leaf out of the cheerful Caribbean's book and discover why Cuban parties are so famous and why visitors often have such a good time. However, I suspected that beneath this sense of energetic sociality a deeper, rather stressful grief marked the lives of almost everyone. People seemed to seek excitement, enjoyment and sociality in part because they felt such experiences were a substitute for other forms of satisfaction, which was partly – but by no means entirely – a result of material poverty that many felt had increased in the wake of the Soviet collapse.

La Lucha

Although not all residents work hard in formal occupations, people would tell me that just to live is hard work; in the Tivolí, life is quite literally seen as a daily battle (*una lucha*). It was this battle, this work, which formed a large part of my fieldwork because it was the dominant activity that marked the lives of my informants. After 50 years of revolution, in which transformations of daily life had occurred in such public activities as education, health care and labor, I was struck by the peripheral status that public life and public work seemed to hold in the activities and consciousnesses of my neighbors. The average Cuban resident characterized his or her quality of life with reference not to universities, hospitals, museums and workplaces, but rather with reference to more localized and less institutional spaces such as street corners, living rooms and food markets. My primary intention in this study was to sketch out the significance of the practices and objects that inhabit such localized and informal spaces, as they form a fundamentally important location for enacting and understanding what it is to be Cuban in the post-Soviet era. To describe the practices that I identify as fundamental to the understanding of this life, I invoke the notion of struggle, inspired by the vernacular use of the verb *luchar*, to struggle or battle, as it is frequently used to define the particular challenges encountered in everyday life. Many of the most common and most problematic struggles of urban residents are related to the acquisition and maintenance of material objects, specifically mass-produced consumer goods. It is through Cubans' struggle to acquire such various commodities as cooking oil, soap, decorative ornaments and televisions that they judge the material and social progress of their own lives and the lives of others, as well as the material and social progress of Cuban society as a whole.

The daily experiences of being a consumer in a society where consumption is largely experienced as frustration and an absence of desirable goods has come for many Cubans to be emblematic of the shifts that Cuba has undergone since 1990, in the post-Soviet economic transformation that is officially and vernacularly described as the "Special Period" (*Periodo Especial*). Two particular moments in history triggered much of what distinguishes the Special Period from the preceding Soviet-influenced configuration of Cuban politics and economy. First, the end of communism in Europe and the collapse of the Soviet Union between 1989-1991 precipitated an unexpected crisis that dramatically reduced the capacity of the Cuban state to deliver both basic and luxury commodities to its citizens.

Second, between 1991 and 1993 in response to this crisis the Cuban government announced a series of economic reforms, which effectively inaugurated a dual economy that, despite changes in currency policy, has been an ongoing feature of Cuban life.[1] These and subsequent economic reforms in the 1990s created a distinctive new kind of Cuban socialism, an unforeseen mixture of socialist and market-driven economic practices very different from the paths of other post-socialist "transition economies" in Europe or Asia. But whereas the starting point of this new and dramatically different phase of the Cuban revolution was fairly clear, whether the Special Period has ended is more difficult to decipher. As the following chapters illustrate, the traumas and adjustments that Cuban consumers underwent in the 1990s have had lasting cultural effects.

different? ✶

Understanding the "Special Period in Times of Peace": Cuba after the Soviet Collapse

When the "Special Period in Times of Peace" was announced in 1990, most Cubans were yet to feel the

---

[1] From 1993 to 2004, US dollars became legal tender in Cuba, but the Cuban peso (*moneda nacional,* or MN) remained the currency used in some state-run shops and markets, and remained the currency in which state workers were paid. In 2004, US dollars were once again banned from use in Cuban transactions, but the Convertible Peso (CUC) is used at a rate fixed to the US dollar instead. Since 2004 therefore despite withdrawing the US dollar as legal tender, Cuba has retained a dual economy as the CUC operates alongside the MN for use in different kinds of purchases, services and transactions.

effects of their country's decreasing support from the soon-to-be ex-socialist bloc. When Gorbachev implemented perestroika in the USSR, Cuban officials became increasingly hostile to the new policies of their previous ally; state rhetoric within Cuba soon shifted from defending socialist Europe to criticizing the dramatic reforms that were sweeping the continent.[2] Compounding the problems Cuba was experiencing as a result of the thaw and subsequent collapse of the USSR, the rest of socialist Europe rapidly dropped trade ties with Cuba, as COMECON, the international economic association for communist states, was dissolved in 1991. Meanwhile, the U.S. government under Presidents Bush and Clinton sought to deepen the economic crisis emerging in Cuba. With the 1992 Torricelli Act and the 1996 Helms Burton Act, the U.S. government strengthened longstanding trade embargoes, prevented third-country subsidiaries of U.S. firms from trading with Cuba, prohibited trade of food and medical supplies, and restricted travel and the sending of remittances to Cuba by U.S. citizens (Gott 2004:303-6).[3] The net effect of the disappearance of old trade partners while the U.S. constrained new ones was devastating: Before 1991, 85% of Cuban trade was with socialist bloc countries, but between 1989 and 1993 trade with the Soviet Union alone declined by over 90% (Pérez 2006:292).

---

[2] For a detailed account of the deterioration of relations between Cuba and the USSR during *perestroika,* see Bain 2005.

[3] In 2004, further trade and travel restrictions were introduced in the lead-up to George W. Bush's successful re-election as President of the United States, some of which were eased in 2009 under the Obama administration.

It is hard to exaggerate the dramatic effect that such a collapse in trade, coupled with the U.S. embargo, had upon the most basic activities of everyday life. Horse-drawn plows replaced tractors, walking or cycling replaced driving and charcoal stoves replaced kerosene burners. Electricity black-outs of six to seven hours a day became routine as power plants could not be fueled or maintained (Eckstein 2003:97). In these and other small but important ways, scarcity and shortage significantly altered the practices of housekeeping in the early 1990s in ways that required more hours of harder work than since the early years of the revolution. Consumer goods such as toothpaste, laundry detergent, canned foods and clothes, all of which had been imported, disappeared from the shops, and with the widespread food shortages nutritional levels plummeted, while prices for food items on the black market skyrocketed. In Santiago de Cuba, these sorts of experiences, described in more detail throughout this book, constituted the traumatic daily practices that have come to be remembered as the "hard years of the Special Period" or "full Special Period" (*los años duros del Periodo Especial; pleno Periodo Especial*), in which new repertoires of practices – many of them adapted from those of previous generations in pre-socialist and even pre-capitalist times – were necessary adjustments to the abject shortage of the commodities and resources that are generally associated with modern urban life.

It was within this context that the Cuban government introduced a series of legislative reforms to combat the deepening crisis. Key areas of the economy were opened to foreign investment, with a particular focus on the tourist and mining sectors. Law 141 legalized certain forms of small business in a bid to control the flourishing black market upon which people increasingly depended. Typical examples of such small businesspeople, known as *cuentapropistas*, included hairdressers, fruit vendors, tailors and pedicab drivers. The U.S. dollar was legalized to facilitate the increased emigrant remittances and the Cuban retail sector was significantly reshaped with the opening of *diplomercado* stores, previously restricted to the diplomatic corps, to the general public. These stores have become commonly known as *la shopping,* and the Cubanization of the English word "shopping" indicates how they are linked for consumers to an imaginary world of capitalist consumption, both in the high quality and high prices of the goods. Such wide-sweeping reforms were originally described as short-term measures to face extreme economic adversity, but have in essence set the structure of the Cuban national economy by establishing patterns of domestic economies in households that characteristically rely on a mixture of legal and illegal low-level wealth generation, emigrant remittances and informal transactions that tap into key areas of the service economy such as tourism. Although a wide-reaching – if under-resourced – infrastructure of social services continues to be provided by the Cuban government, the nation's conversion to reliance on tourism and remittances actually presents a model of economic growth that is typically Caribbean. The path that Cuba took in the 1990s, unlike other socialist and post-socialist countries, not only seemed at odds with traditional socialist theory that informed previous decades of economic policy, but seemed to echo a capitalist past with an irony or discomfort that is keenly felt by many Cubans.

Since the beginning of the millennium, the Cuban economy has recovered some degree of stability. Nevertheless, these key adaptations made during the 1990s have become ongoing features of the Cuban economy, in turn shaping the typical patterns of livelihood and domestic practices on which Cubans depend to make daily life manageable. Initiated in the 1990s, the regular and open use of black markets, a dependence upon remittances, and a desire to tap into service sectors such as tourism to access foreign currency are increasingly standard pathways for economic security in urban communities. As a result, everyday life in Santiago de Cuba has brought people into contact with Cubans or foreigners living in capitalist economies, and the borders of Cuba – never hermetically sealed from the cultural influences of the broader Americas – are more regularly crossed by people, currency, media, and cultural practices. Cubans have for almost 20 years lived with the daily effects of this juxtaposition of socialist policies and the global capitalist market, navigating a dual economy and offsetting shortages of state goods and services with other strategies for consumption. By the 1990s, one third of Cubans were in regular contact with friends or family in the United States and the Cuban diaspora had been reinvented through public discourse from traitors who abandoned the socialist revolution to brothers and sisters in international solidarity (Eckstein 2003:120). Thus, by 2002 remittances formed an estimated 70% of dollars informally obtained by Cubans. Those who in previous times might have played down their family connections abroad now proudly display photographs in their living rooms of daughters in Rome, or uncles in Miami, and it is common knowledge that maintaining good relationships with relatives abroad is the primary method of ensuring economic survival in contemporary Cuba.

For Cuban residents in cities such as Santiago de Cuba, the net result of the economic transformation of Cuba has been that income discrepancies and social differentiation have increased in comparison to the Soviet socialist decades of the 1960s –1980s. Although remittance economies in other parts of the Caribbean where income discrepancies are high tend to reduce income differentials, in Cuba it has had the opposite effect. By the late 1990s the estimated disparity in income between poorest and richest Cubans had gone from 4:1 to 25:1 (Eckstein 2003: 234-5; Pérez 2006:312). Race and class have reemerged as telling indicators of social status to a degree that was less apparent during Soviet socialism. Despite the popular image within Cuba of young, largely black delinquents benefiting from the Special Period emergence of prostitution, tourist hustling and crime (Holbraad 2004, Rundle 2006), statistically the Cubans most likely to have prospered seem to be overwhelmingly white. Susan Eckstein argues that in both tourism and remittances white Cubans are the most likely to gain (at least through official income generation). Ninety-six percent of the Cuban American community, the largest source of remittances, identify as white, and white Cubans hold approximately 80% of dollar-economy jobs within Cuba (Eckstein 2003:233). Perhaps in recognition of the growing discrepancies between citizens that seem so antithetical to typical socialist aims, the Cuban government

Class

re-racializ

96% of Cub. Am. ID as white

has signaled a shift away from reliance on the dollar economy by introducing measures to limit the impact of tourism on everyday life in Cuba and to regain control of small business in which dollars legally and illegally circulate. Most notably, in November 2004 the U.S. dollar was once again prohibited as legal tender within Cuba. Citizens possessing dollars had to exchange them at the government-set rate of 90 U.S. cents for 1 Cuban convertible peso, effectively raising by 10% the prices of all consumer goods available through the *shopping* stores. Despite such price rises, in 2008 and 2010 Raúl Castro announced two sets of reforms aimed to quell consumer dissatisfaction with the ongoing lack of certain goods and to address concerns about the effects of the 2008-2009 global financial crisis on Cuba's economy.

Economists, political scientists, historians and media commentators have compiled a substantial narrative of this transformation of Cuba that documents a fascinating complex of national concerns and transnational pressures, pragmatic strategies and ideological principles, institutional structures and charismatic individuals (Pérez 2006; Eckstein 2003; Morris 2008; Chávez 2005). The social effects of this transition are equally compelling, judging from emerging international and multidisciplinary scholarship of the culture of the Special Period, of which this book is a part. The Special Period forged new kinds of art, music, and literature, in turn opening new roles for cultural producers in Cuban society and transnational creative industries (Hernández Reguant 2002; Fernandes 2003; Whitfield 2008). New kinds of relationships – romantic, professional, familial – have been analyzed by

Shortages ob definitive ob the SP

anthropologists as has the renegotiated role of a Cuban civil society and the new possibilities, and distinct dissatisfactions, of citizenship that this society presents (Fernández 1999; Settle 2007; Rundle 2001; Hearn 2008; Rosenberg Weinreb 2007). Through many of these approaches to understanding post-Soviet Cuba, there is acknowledgment of the role that consumption – and a decline in opportunities for consumption – has played in everyday life since the mid-1990s. It is the central argument of this book that for Cubans themselves the shortages and scarcities of the Special Period have become a definitive – if not the definitive – experience through which their quotidian practices, domestic spaces, personal relationships and even their place in Cuban history, are negotiated and understood. Although the diversity and quality of commodities available through the dual economy have substantially improved the material conditions of most households since the peak of the crisis in 1993-1994, the overwhelming majority of Cubans remain dissatisfied with the possibilities for consumption available to them. Most are acutely aware of the absence of consumer goods in their shops and view consumer opportunities in Cuba negatively in comparison with the past and with contemporary societies elsewhere in the world. Discussions about what life was like "before" (*antes*), whether this means before the Cuban revolution or before the economic crisis triggered by the collapse of the Soviet Union and deepened by U.S. hostility, often focus on the superior groceries and commodities that were available in shops and markets. Of course, in reality there have been experiences of scarcity by some sectors of the nation across all periods of Cuban history. The early momentum of the Cuban revolution was largely focused on addressing scarcity through the redistribution of resources. More recently, various sources document that even the most prosperous periods of Soviet Cuba were accompanied by complaints about queues and shortages (Galeano 1997:77; Rosendahl 1997:38-9).[4] But such historical perspectives do not alter the contemporary perception of scarcity as being definitive of the post-Soviet era, and this perception is intensified by the more frequent comparisons that Cubans are making between their material status and what seem to be better material worlds abroad, *en el extranjero*. Conversations about life abroad commonly center on the diversity, quality and quantity of consumer items offered; clothes, food and technologies ranging from cars to mobile phones to domestic appliances

---

[4] Swedish anthropologist Mona Rosendahl's excellent ethnography of a small Cuban town in the mid to late 1980s documents that, although some consumers found the cost of living high, basic expenses were manageable even on lower salaries. Discussing consumer attitudes in the late 1980s, Rosendahl notes a dissatisfaction that was rather different from the situation experienced by Cubans some five years later: "Many people have more money than they can spend. This is in part why dissatisfaction with the lack of available goods is probably the most common complaint that people in Palmera express about their life situations" (Rosendahl 1997:35). Sociologist Susan Eckstein uses government data to suggest that people were also generally dissatisfied with consumer prices and a high cost of living in 1990, just before the severe economic crisis had an impact at everyday level (Eckstein 2003:119-120). Nevertheless, while consumers expressed dissatisfaction during the 1980s, which Rosendahl attributes to an excess of spending money and a relative shortage of goods, by 2004, my informants in Santiago looked back upon that period as an era of plenty. Clearly, consumer dissatisfaction does have strong socialist antecedents, but it is not constructed as such by many Cubans today, for whom shortage has become predominantly associated with the Special Period.

dominate such discussions. Foreign visitors and Cubans who have worked or traveled abroad are frequent sources of stories and opinions about consumer opportunities to be enjoyed not only in the United States, which might be expected to be the paradigmatic example of *el extranjero*, but also in such diverse places as Spain, Jamaica, Russia, Venezuela and Angola. Along with films, videos, visits and updates from relatives and friends living overseas, such imagined worlds are evoked by the increased presence of tourists, usually from Western Europe or North America, enjoying holidays that rarely represent the nature of their everyday lives at home. For Cubans *el extranjero* is an imaginary place representing all that is the opposite of life "here and now" under socialism, much as anthropologist Alexei Yurchak described "the West" that was imagined by the last generation of Soviet citizens (Yurchak 2005).

Socialist Consumer Culture? Cuban Consumption in the Soviet Era

There are other historical factors that help explain why Cuban citizens would tie their measure of wellbeing so closely to the availability and quality of mass-produced goods. Certainly, the trauma of sudden scarcity in the 1990s was intensified by the period of relative abundance that immediately preceded it, and by recognition by the socialist government that opportunities for consumption and access to consumer goods should be enhanced. Of course, Cuban socialism – officially declared state practice in 1961, two years after revolutionary forces ousted

Fulgencio Batista from leadership – has moved through distinct, and at times contradictory, phases of political and economic transition so that socialism in Cuba was reformulated to fit changing domestic, international, economic and political pressures. Cycles of restructuring the Cuban economy moved from aborted attempts at rapid industrialization in the early 1960s, back to a central dependence on sugar exports in the late 1960s, into a deepening alliance with and dependence on the Soviet Union in the 1970s and early 1980s. But as economic and workplace reforms were made and re-made, a principal area in which citizens experienced change was in their access to consumer goods, as rationing systems and workplace incentive schemes were variously introduced, withdrawn and reintroduced. The decades from the 1960s to 1980s (which I refer to as the Soviet period, although the extent of Sovietization throughout this period fluctuated) seemed to be an ongoing experiment of adjusting measures of workplace and consumer reform against incentive schemes exploiting the desire for greater income and consumer goods in order to spur productivity (Eckstein 2003:39-47).

Just one example of the role of consumer goods in the Soviet era is the 1970s workplace subsidization scheme "Plan CTC," [5] through which 100,000 televisions were distributed to leading workers in 1973 (Pérez 2006: 265-70). Throughout the 1970s and early 1980s, a Cuban professional class began acquiring high-status household

---

[5] CTC is an acronym for the *Central de Trabajadores de Cuba,* the "Cuban Workers' Federation". The impact of the Plan CTC upon the material culture of households is discussed in Chapter 4.

goods through a combination of workplace incentives and installment and savings plans (see for example Rosendahl 1997:36-7; Eckstein 2003:56). Shifts in workplace and salary structure and consumer policy seemed to stimulate the economy and increase the supply and availability of consumer goods. For several households in this study, that period is now remembered as a golden era of material acquisition, and the legacy of domestic appliances, furniture and home furnishings purchased or "earned" during this period continue to be important in the house and home today.

Socialist societies have often been represented as being "anti-consumption," or at least as the opposite of the hedonistic excesses of capitalist consumer cultures, and socialist consumers across the world have often identified socialist societies as being cultures of shortages (Verdery 1996). And yet, in certain times and places, citizens of socialist societies participated in a transnational socialist consumer culture encouraged by governing regimes, whether by a socialist aesthetic in domestic décor, the marketing of luxury goods such as champagne and caviar, or by the symbolic role that modern domestic appliances played in the Cold War (Reid & Crowley 2000, Gronow 2003, Oldenziel & Zachman 2009). In Cuba, the decades immediately preceding the Special Period were a period in which a "good life," including the material comforts of modernity, seemed attainable for a significant portion of the population, making the transition to serious shortages in food, fuel and basic services within a three-year period seem all the more shocking.

The Historical Context of Cuban Consumption

The Cuban experience of socialist consumption is different from that of other countries because Cuba had a long pre-revolutionary history of Western (and often U.S.) consumer goods as part of everyday life. By the 1950s Cuba had one of the largest middle-class populations in Latin America and the Caribbean, whose material culture and lifestyle were similar to that of middle-class U.S. Americans (Gott 2005:165). Radio, film and television were pioneered in Cuba before taking off in other Latin American markets, and all were deeply tied to U.S. media industries, so that popular culture and the aesthetics of Cuban consumption were firmly rooted in a nascent U.S. American consumer culture; rather than describing modern Cuba as having been "Americanized," it is more the case that elite and middle-class Cubans were involved in pan-American consumer culture.[6] In doing so, Cuban consumers integrated U.S. American goods into their everyday lives as another iteration of their centuries-long involvement in global networks of commodities. This history is shared with the rest of the Caribbean region, which has been identified by a number of scholars as a birthplace or incubator for the transnational social and economic arrangements that grew to become characteristic of modernity. The early annihilation of indigenous communities, the forced creation

---

[6] Nor was such consumption restricted entirely to the metropoles; in a treatise that has inspired many Latin American scholars of modernity, Eduardo Galeano notes that as early as 1859 a Spanish traveler reported finding US-made Singer sewing machines in a remote Cuban village (1997:71).

of new, African diaspora communities and the arrival of migrants, traders and indentured laborers from Europe, America and Asia all led to the rise of new combinations of social forms with minimal reference to historical tradition, so that in the Caribbean the concept of tradition largely succeeded the presence of modernity (Trouillot 1992). European migrants, slave traders and plantation owners, African slave populations, Franco-Haitian refugees, Chinese laborers and other groups of people came to and went from Cuba through the centuries. This is an economic and political history in which not only people and ideas, but also material products, were agents of social change. By the nineteenth century, the Caribbean and much of Latin America were firmly integrated into "import economies that linked the objects of everyday life in Latin American communities to the structures of global capitalism" (Orlove & Bauer 1997:234-68).

It has often been noted that the development of export industries such as sugar, tobacco and coffee was not only significant in shaping Cuban history and culture and Caribbean regional economies, but opened the way for the modern development of global capitalism and transformed the daily practices of consumers in Europe and across the world (Mintz 1986, Ortiz 1973, Stubbs 1985, Galeano 1997:67). Cuban coffee and sugar industries, which both reached their peak in the nineteenth century resulting the wake of the Haitian revolution, generated tremendous wealth and an elite community of growers and traders in Cuba who were able to import the latest fashionable goods from around the world (Galeano 1997:67; Carlson 2009). But imports in everyday life were not merely for the rich;

there is considerable historical evidence that shows generally that poorer communities in the Caribbean were more engaged in trading than agriculture or manufacturing. The structure of Caribbean sugar-plantation economies in the nineteenth century, and their reorganization in the early twentieth century under U.S. administration, made small landholders a tiny minority of the rural population and an agricultural labor force rather than an autonomous farming community. These farmers were described by historian Sidney Mintz as "landless, property-less, wage-earning, and store-buying" (Mintz 1974:62). Staple diets in the Caribbean region have long relied on imports ranging from salt-beef from Ireland in the seventeenth century to the imported ingredients that formed new kinds of "national cuisines" in the nineteenth and twentieth centuries (Mandelblatt 2007, Wilk 2006, Pertierra 2011).

Such a brief outline of Cuban history sketches a background for an essential point upon which my own study of consumption in twenty-first century Cuba is based. In short: Cuba has a long involvement in global circuits of goods and capital, and is far from an undeveloped or new consumer society. The crisis of consumption that has troubled Cubans is a result of their longstanding dependence on global networks of imported commodities for basic everyday activities related to food, hygiene and housing, and this was no less true of Cuba during the Soviet era than in previous periods of modern history. In Cuba, despite failed attempts in the 1960s to diversify the national economy, the transition from capitalism to socialism was largely experienced by consumers as a change in the *origins* of consumer goods; there was not much change to a longstanding reliance on imports to maintain everyday life, so that what was effectively a transition from an American satellite to a Soviet dependant did not cause a fundamental shift in how "foreign" versus "local" goods were socially constructed. Cuban consumers were in a different position from Russians and East Germans, for whom socialist goods were seen – for better or worse – to be specifically local (cf. Humphrey 1995; Caldwell 2004).[7] In contrast, Cuban consumers, whether under socialism or capitalism, always incorporated foreign goods as essentially "local" components of everyday life, and are thoroughly used to inclusion in global circuits of cross-cultural production and consumption. Despite Cuba's symbolic and political role as an example of freedom from the tyranny of U.S. involvement in everyday life, the political and economic support of the Soviet Union determined basic wellbeing of Cubans, and the difficult consequences of the Soviet collapse is indicative of the degree to which Cuba remains deeply ensconced in postcolonial legacies of *las Américas*.

 foreign goods as essentially local components of everyday life

---

[7] In a rather different cultural context, Vann has found that Vietnamese consumers are also very concerned to distinguish between local and imported goods, because the proliferation under "market socialism" of locally produced goods has not been accompanied by a growing consumer confidence in such goods as authentic or appealing (Vann 2005).

Consumption Matters

I have suggested some of the reasons why in Cuba (as in many industrialized societies), pleasure and desire are so frequently configured around activities of consumption. Mass-produced commodities are consciously prioritized as central to what social scientists have described as social reproduction; the transmission and renewal of social and economic order.[8] To live well in Cuba, and to demonstrate that one is living well, requires wearing good clothes, eating at restaurants, being impeccably groomed and sharing generously with loved ones. As is often the case, the tastes and identities expressed through such consumer choices form the basis for important moral debates, as excessively conspicuous or excessively frugal forms of consumption can be lauded or decried for their moral implications (Wilk 2001). However the sort of consumption I focus on is not the conspicuous consumption so often the subject of moral debates, but rather the more banal consumption practices that are of significance largely because they should be so pedestrian. Even without living well, merely to live "normally" in Cuba requires access to a range of commodities regarded as necessities; not only food and shelter, but also refrigerators that allow food to be

---

[8] I use the term "social reproduction" in its most basic sense, to mean the renewal of social, political and economic order (Barnard & Spencer 1996:622). Although Marxist anthropologists often focused on the role of labor as a process that enabled social reproduction, I argue (following many others, including consumption scholars mentioned in this Introduction) that the processes of consumption are just as important.

preserved in a tropical climate and access to entertainment and information through media technologies.

Anthropologists have long been interested in the relationships that are developed between people and objects, and in the comparative conditions of alienable and inalienable goods that seem to lie at the heart of any investigation into production, consumption or distribution (see for example Malinowski 1960; Mauss 1990; Appadurai 1986). Theories of exchange, of the gift and of the role of commodities, although sometimes developed in reference to societies not known for their consumerism, have raised the question similar to one more recently considered by anthropologists studying mass consumption in large-scale market economies: How are relationships between people expressed and negotiated through the transfer of goods? The use of ethnography to research industrialized urban communities and increasing mass consumption, even in remote communities for whom market economies are recent, has produced anthropology that examines the impact and meaning of consumer goods and vast networks of global production and consumption (cf. Miller 1987; Bourdieu 1984; Miller 1995; Orlove 1997; Howes 1996; Foster 2002; McCracken 1988).

Despite – or rather because of – Cuba's history of consumption, as an example it calls attention to the consequences that global economics have upon local and national communities, and suggests that studying global consumption must include the social creation of scarcity. Through identifying their lives as lacking crucial commodities, Cubans are demonstrating their deep immersion in the contemporary consumer culture. As such, this ethnography is an example of what James Ferguson has called the "anthropology of decline," the role of consumption in communities that were once on their way to increasing affluence, but have subsequently been altered by severe economic downturns (Ferguson 1999; see also Burke 1996; Newman 1988; Goody 1982; O'Dougherty 2002; Drakúlic 1992; Humphrey 1995). We can only imagine that the current global financial crisis will lead to overdue attention to these cultures because the Cuban example and others show that the importance of consumption does not decrease in periods of downward mobility. On the contrary, in times of economic crisis consumption becomes more important as it occupies greater proportions of people's time and money (Goody 1982:175-90; Newman 1988 95-113).

Although it remains to be seen whether Cuban policymakers will deliver on their early-1990s promise that the Special Period measures are a temporary suspension of socialist economics, the transition of the Cuban presidency in 2006-2008, from Fidel to Raúl Castro, has reinforced a sense among Cubans that the Special Period was not, as suggested by some outside commentators, the first phase of an inevitable transition toward capitalist democracy. Rather, Cuba in the twenty-first century has seen the first generation of citizens grow up in a post-Soviet system; both isolated from and connected to products and practices of the broader world. For people in the struggle of everyday life in contemporary Cuba, the disjuncture between the socialist rhetoric and seemingly non-socialist practices of the state is negotiated with a spectrum of responses ranging from frustration or even outrage to weary resignation and good-humored acceptance.

A Guide to the Chapters

This book focuses on people and the places and spaces in which consumption coping skills are practiced. Chapter 1 introduces the city of Santiago de Cuba, and the neighborhood of the Tivolí through the stories of the research participants whose conversations with me form an important part of this book. In describing their life stories, their households and the neighborhood in which most live, I also consider some of the methodological issues of ethnographic research in urban Cuba.

Chapter 2 considers three key practices that define post-Soviet Cuban life: struggle (*luchar*), invention (*inventar*) and acquisition (*conseguir*). In this chapter I also explain their discursive significance in everyday conversation and in the public discourses of revolutionary history and mass media. Chapter 3 turns to the practices of shopping for groceries, by no means a set of simple activities in contemporary economy. Although the sheer number of hours taken up with shopping is reason enough to consider the practices, I also examine how the burden of shopping and homemaking have especially affected women, who assume primary responsibility for domestic management and economy.

In Chapter 4, the focus on the home extends to an analysis of domestic material culture. By examining the contents of several houses and the ways by which they were acquired, I show the centrality of furnishings, décor and domestic technologies to the sense of quality of life for Cuban citizens. Home contents reveal sustained and multiple paths of commodities sourced globally as well as locally, which were by no means curtailed with socialism.

Moving away from the Tivolí and to more recent networks of research informants, Chapter 5 considers the changing landscape of media consumption in Santiago de Cuba. I contrast the prominent role of mass media in the development of the Cuban revolution with the more ambivalent status of new media and information and communication technologies. As in other chapters, focus is on the everyday practices of consumption rather than on policy or economic analysis or political critique, which are well represented in the broader field of Cuban studies. In the Conclusion, I consider what this approach might offer to the broader field, with a particular eye toward Cuba's future.

Chapter 1

Life in the Tivolí: *A Neighborhood in Santiago de Cuba*

Throughout this study, I include interviews with a number of people, most of who lived in the neighborhood known informally as *El Tivolí*, an old central neighborhood in Cuba's second largest city, Santiago de Cuba.

Fig. 1 *The Padre Pico steps in the Tivolí*

The Tivolí takes up approximately 40 irregular hilly blocks on the southeast side of the historical center of Santiago de Cuba, on the fringes of the city's oldest plaza. The randomly colored houses that perch along the city hillsides stand out against the dark green of the mountains and the bright blue sky, so typical of the hot, still days for which Santiago is known. On the opposite side of the Santiago de Cuba Bay, clearly visible from the Tivolí, lie industrial plants that service the province: a concrete factory, rum and beer distilleries, and assorted Soviet-designed complexes pointed out to tourists with pride as symbols of socialist development. The main streets of the Tivolí follow the crest of the first hills above the bay around which Santiago de Cuba was built. The hilly landscape of the city begins near the Tivolí, with dense and colorful architecture largely dating from the Spanish colonial era of the eighteenth and nineteenth centuries, and spreads outward incorporating upscale neighborhoods built in the 1930s, suburban developments for the middle-class population of the 1950s, and further outlying housing projects inspired by Soviet brutalism. In many areas, these architectural legacies coexist with improvised concrete constructions. This is certainly the case in the Tivolí. Although a few wooden shacks remain, approximately two thirds of the houses were rebuilt in concrete over the past 50 years, empty lots filled and larger houses divided that were originally built to accommodate the families of the local bourgeoisie (Del Real & Pertierra, 2008).

Although the Tivolí is not an especially prosperous neighborhood, the material conditions of even the poorest houses are substantially better than those of the urban poor elsewhere in Latin America. Virtually all have electricity, indoor plumbing, a toilet that is indoors or in an inside patio, and several rooms. In poorer apartments that are subdivisions of larger spaces, toilets may be shared between two or three households. Although the maintenance of basic urban infrastructure is inconsistent in Santiago de Cuba, all houses do rely on citywide services such as garbage collection, water, electricity and public-health services such as fumigation and water-tank inspections.

The Tivolí has slightly fewer than 6,000 registered residents,[9] although my own research suggests that the significant number of unregistered residents increases the population by as much as 25%. Within Santiago de Cuba, residents of the Tivolí (usually known as *Tivoliceros*) have a reputation for being devoted to their community and deeply involved in the musical and Carnival traditions for which the city is known. The Tivolí is sometimes said to be a "bad" neighborhood (*un barrio malo*), full of disreputable people, thieves and drunkards. This view was often refuted by residents who countered that theirs was a neighborhood in which everybody knew each other, and where people looked after their own, even if they were willing to take advantage of outsiders. The complex politics of race that characterizes Cuba is particularly apparent in Santiago, a city whose population is majority non-white, and there is an essential (but generally unspoken) allusion to race at the source of the Tivolí's ambiguous reputation as both a dangerous space and an important repository of Afro-

bad neighborhood

race

---

[9] Estimate provided by the *Dirección Municipal de Planificación Física, Departamento de Información de Santiago de Cuba*. This extremely rough estimate is drawn from 1999 census data (at the time of fieldwork, 2002 census data had not yet been released). The estimate is inadequate because, in addition to measuring only the number of residents officially listed in local households, it is drawn from the populations of three separate census zones, each of which form part of the area informally known as the Tivolí.

Cuban culture.[10] Despite the popular image of the Tivolí as a predominantly Afro-Cuban community, many white families live in the area, and a few are the children or grandchildren of the bourgeoisie who remained in Cuba after the revolution. Steady waves of urbanization since the revolution have brought many white and mixed race families from impoverished rural areas across Eastern Cuba, so that the white residents of the Tivolí today – several of whom are profiled below – are more often the children of *guajiros,* descended from Spanish migrants and raised in rural poverty than the children of middle-class families, although a few such households do remain. Although the public identity of the Tivolí as a notorious neighborhood had little impact on the direction and findings of my research, it is worth briefly noting how and why such an identity came into being. The sense of pride that many of my informants took in belonging to the Tivolí certainly contributed to the enthusiasm with which my research was generally received, and recognition of the area's special contribution to the history and culture of Santiago was important in making it an attractive place to begin fieldwork in the first place.

---

[10] The ambivalence with which Tivolíceros are regarded by other people in Santiago is echoed at a national level in representations of people from Santiago and other people from Eastern Cuba (*Orientales*) as all that is both good and bad about Afro-Cuba (Moore 1997:220). Santiago is said to be the heart of black Cuba, from which important political and cultural traditions have emerged. But Santiagueros are frequently characterized by other Cubans as dangerous, untrustworthy and dishonorable.

A Franco-Haitian Neighborhood

The growth of the Tivolí at the beginning of the nineteenth century was largely prompted by the settlement of Haitians and Franco-Haitians in Cuba in the wake of the Haitian revolution. By 1803, about 32,000 Haitians had sought refuge in the Oriente region, principally in Santiago de Cuba and Baracoa (Marrero 1983:143-50).[11] Several of the grandest buildings in the Tivolí were built by wealthy Franco-Haitians who went to on develop coffee plantations in the nearby mountains, but many less wealthy refugees, including *criollos*, free black Haitians, slaves and domestic servants also relocated to the area (Padrón 1997; Marrero 1983:150). Subsequent waves of migration from France and a prosperous economy elevated the community into prominence, and the name *El Tivolí* is said to derive from a famous café that was established in the neighborhood during its heyday. The performers who graced the stages of the café seem to have left less of a mark on the cultural practices of contemporary Tivoliceros than the Afro-Haitians whose societies and drumming sessions (known as

---

[11] The area was never exclusively Haitian or Franco-Haitian; for example, "Arabs" (probably Lebanese traders) were also said to have lived in the Tivolí since its beginnings. As Spanish subjects only were permitted to live within the walls of the official city, the Tivolí's position between the port and the city perimeter became something of an enclave for prosperous foreigners. In 1809 in response to the installation of Joseph Bonaparte as King of Spain, a tide of anti-French sentiment prompted many Franco-Haitian refugees to leave Cuba, but many more became naturalized Spanish subjects or left temporarily only to return to their business interests in Santiago de Cuba after Bonaparte's abdication. (Marrero 1983:150).

tumba francesa) were integral to development of the musical traditions of *conga* and the *comparsas* that remain a highlight of the Santiago Carnival season (Alén Rodriguez 1991; Bettelheim 1991). However, beyond the historical identity of the Tivolí as being "French," rich in folklore and strongly involved in Afro-Caribbean cultural practices, few events of daily life mark Tivolíceros as different from other contemporary urban Cubans. Although French surnames are common in Santiago (as they are across southeastern Cuba where Haitian migration was concentrated), in general, people in the Tivolí eat the same food, speak the same language and engage in the same daily practices as other Cuban citizens.

Tourists regularly walk through the Tivolí, usually to visit the local museum (described in Chapter 2), to enjoy the view of the bay, or to listen to traditional music at the *Casa de las Tradiciones* (a community music hall). Several residents with well-maintained and spacious houses have licenses to rent rooms to tourists. A local dance troupe conducts regular dance workshops and performances for tourist groups, and an illegal but longstanding restaurant operates from an innocuous-looking house in one corner of the neighborhood. It would seem that at least some residents and institutions in the Tivolí have benefited from the boost of legal and illegal income that tourism has brought to Cuba. However, not a few residents spoke to me of the problems they feel have resulted from a tourist economy. Apart from feeling that their own lives rarely benefited from, and were sometimes inconvenienced by, the presence of tourists, many older people spoke of the need to "rescue the values" of the Cuban revolution as increasing numbers of young people dropped out of school and salaried work to focus their energies on earning dollars through informal means such as hustling tourists and sexual relationships with foreigners (cf. Rundle 2001).

energy focused on earning dollars

Neighborhoods or Communities: A Challenge for Urban Anthropology?

A skeptical reader may wonder whether the picture presented here of a bounded space to which residents identify as belonging is the sort of literary device for which anthropologists have been known, fostering an image of a contained, isolated set of people who can easily be termed a "community." But everyday practices in urban neighborhoods like the Tivolí, as well as the role of the neighborhood in Santiago's history, do genuinely reinforce a relationship between inhabitants and their immediate vicinity. Many of the challenges identified by anthropologists in studying unbounded heterogeneous modern urban communities are minimized in urban Cuba by the degree to which daily life takes place within a local area that is generally walking distance from one's house (Cornelius 1974:9; Low 1996; Miller 2006). The least independent members of the community – usually the very young and the very old – rarely leave the neighborhood at all. Numerous medical services, schools, shops and markets are within walking distance, if not within the Tivolí proper, and the area's proximity to Santiago's historical center

most places walking distance

enables residents to regularly use the city's main shopping district and government offices with relative ease.[12]

Fig. 2 *Santiago's main shopping street*

---

[12] Within approximately 30 minutes walk from the Tivolí, residents have access to 25 medical services and 11 schools. Important shopping areas (with goods sold both Cuban currencies are located less than 15 minutes' walk, and two agricultural markets (of which only one lies in the central historical district) are also reached in less than half an hour's walk. For residents unwilling or unable to navigate steep hills and constant heat on a regular basis, the majority of daily chores can be completed within the Tivolí itself. Rations are collected from State outlets that typically service areas of around 20 blocks, and family doctors' practices are similarly allocated, with two practices servicing the majority of Tivolí residents. The neighborhood includes two primary schools and a secondary school, although students are not obliged to attend their nearest school and may travel some distance to attend specialised schools, even boarding for senior secondary education.

Food and grocery items, whether allocated as low-cost rations or bought at higher prices in dollar stores, can be supplemented by the various legal street-food vendors, by informal networks of black market goods and by traveling vendors who walk regular routes through the Tivolí selling cooked food, fresh produce and domestic items such as brooms. During Carnival, the Tivolí's main street has for many years been an important venue for people from around the city to visit, and just beyond the southernmost end of the Tivolí is the street known as *Trocha*, which sees one of the city's biggest Carnival gatherings of people and musicians every year. At quieter times, many Tivolí residents (especially men) use the facilities of the three small parks in the area to rest and chat, or they simply spread onto footpaths and street corners to socialize, play dominoes, drink rum and talk about baseball or boxing.

Therefore, although this community is part of a larger urban environment, residents tend to shop, cook, study, care for families and socialize in or near their homes, if only to avoid the difficulties involved in departing from the neighborhood.

dwelling

Across Cuba, state structures are firmly rooted in local neighborhood life through the presence of such institutions as the Committee for the Defense of the Revolution or CDR (*Comité de Defensa de la Revolución*), in which each block (or in rural areas, each village) forms an association led by an elected committee that oversees the wellbeing of residents. Some activities relate to the dispersal of goods and services (such as distributing lids for water tanks to

market argument for the importance of place

Fig. 3 *Shopping for second-hand clothes*

Fig. 4 *A manicure business within a city store*

keep mosquitoes out, or petitioning local authorities to repair community property). Other functions of the CDR are to maintain vigilance against crime and counter-revolutionary activity, to protect CDR members from harm and to ensure that members maintain at least an apparent commitment to the revolution.[13] Another nationwide institution structured at the neighborhood level is the *Federación de Mujeres Cubanas* (Federation of Cuban Women) or FMC, intended to bring the institutions of the revolution to the everyday sphere of the many women who were not salaried workers and therefore not involved in labor unions. Although almost all residents of the Tivolí are nominally members of their local CDR and (for women) FMC units, these organizations have declined in significance and activity since the 1990s and typically depend on a few committed neighbors to take up executive positions. While the CDR and FMC have declined in influence, there is an increasing presence of non-governmental civic groups, such as religious groups and folkloric associations, creating other spaces in which

---

[13] The latter function of the CDR has received great attention in international commentary on the repressive capacity of the Cuban state, but my own experience very much confirms observations made by Douglas Butterworth more than twenty years earlier, that the focus on CDRs as effective vehicles of surveillance is exaggerated, and in practice many CDRs wax and wane in their effectiveness according to the degree of state encouragement, the personal dynamics of committee members, the constituency of the neighborhood, and the nature of practices dominating CDR activities (Butterworth 1974). The moments at which CDRs seemed to spring into life and be of interest to residents of the Tivolí were the times at which block parties were being planned or goods were being distributed. At other times, some residents saw attending CDR meetings as a chore to be endured or avoided as inconspicuously as possible, although other residents were also known for their vigorous contribution to such meetings.

people come together in search of social, spiritual and practical support.

Life Stories from the Tivolí: Los Tivoliceros

One of the easiest ways to begin to understand the complex – and often seemingly contradictory – belief systems, practices and strategies that Cubans use in daily life is to introduce the individuals whose stories are integral to this research. The project included participant observation among networks of households and neighbors, totaling around 70 individuals; a survey of 40 households; and interviews with scholars, government employees and representatives of community organizations. But it is often particular people, and particular stories, that best capture aspects of Cuban consumption and material culture. Reading about individual lives is certainly a pleasant counterbalance to the dense theory and heavy referencing for which academic writing is known. Much of this project was developed as part of a broader initiative to deliberately return to the consideration of individual people and ground-level ethnographic detail as opposed to a broader trend of focus on abstract theory, which has characterized recent anthropological scholarship (cf. Miller 2009). A focus on the experiences and practices of individual people, differently located within social structures, harnesses the strength of ethnography as an approach to study the world, opening up anthropological writing to wider audiences. Without necessarily simplifying the analyses of culture, individual people and their stories, examples and observed behaviors are more than mere illustrations of a deeper theoretical argument.

As a foreign researcher navigating my way through Cuba, I needed to balance the genuine relationships and productive exchanges I enjoyed with my research participants against a concern that my work if carelessly presented might create problems for them. Although I never experienced surveillance or hostility about my activities in Santiago de Cuba, permission for foreigners to do research or study in Cuba is conditional on their engaging in work that is, at the very least, not hostile to the principles that form the basis of the political system. A central part of my argument is that in areas of consumption, people's complaints are not necessarily a complaint against the Cuban government or the legitimacy of its founding principles. However, it is quite possible to use everyday accounts of openly expressed dissatisfaction in a way that misconstrues the criticism. Rather than eliminate any reference to actual people in actual places, or turn to fiction or autobiography, my strategy was to develop my analysis with reference to a wide range of field notes and conversations, and to publish the exchanges and accounts only with the consent of participants. The presence of a data recorder during semi-structured interviews, far from inhibiting our conversations in some way clarified them, as people understood when we were talking for "my work," and when we were talking "off the record," even if my overall analysis draws from both.

Although individual stories presented here draw from interviews as much as from participant observation, this project is not an oral history, *testimonio,* a narrative of life stories, or a compilation of interview transcripts. My observations of individuals are filtered through my impressions of them, and the case studies are chosen because they best highlight broader arguments in this study. But above and beyond stylistic, methodological and ethical concerns, introducing some of the people whose lives informed my study is the most honest reflection of my own path to processing the role of consumption in post-Soviet Cuba. More than merely "informing" my ideas, the practices and objects I encountered through knowing people in Santiago de Cuba are the foundation of this book.

Fernanda

Fernanda is in her late 60s and comes from a poor white rural family.[14] Fernanda is proud to declare that although she had only reached seventh grade, it was seventh grade "of those times," which counted for a lot more than it does today. Fernanda is certainly literate and highly numerate,

---

[14] The dynamics of racial identity in Cuba are complex, and while some readers may question the need to specify an individual's race, to a Cuban specialist it would seem even odder not to. I have written about these people using the basic identifiers Cubans themselves would use to describe someone; name, sex, race and age. However, the spectrum of racial categories Cubans use in identifying themselves and others is enormous, and one person's racial descriptor can vary according to opinion or context, so that someone who identifies as "white,"for example, is by others identified as *mestizo* or *mulatto,* the latter term remaining prevalent in vernacular Cuban. I have ascribed the racial categories to each person presented in this book that I most often heard used in reference to them – noting the one case, Tomasito, which was the least definitive.

and in the past year has attended the *Universidad de Adultos Mayores* (University of Older Adults), a community general education program held on Saturdays for local residents over 60. Fernanda relished becoming a university graduate a few years ago, and she graduated in a formal ceremony with her neighbors in attendance at the provincial theatre.

When Fernanda married over 25 years ago, she moved into her husband's family house in the Tivolí, and after a few years they managed to build a home on top of the existing house for Fernanda, her husband and their two children. The house is made of concrete, painted a cheerful yellow on the outside and sits on the main street of the neighborhood in the block known as *el corazón del Tivolí* (the heart of the Tivolí). The permanent members of the household are Fernanda, her retired husband, her daughter (who identifies as a housewife but who also does manicures and hairstyling for neighbors), her daughter's two daughters (one is a high-school student and the other a social worker) and her son, who spends long periods working in a military camp several hundred kilometers away. Her son's girlfriend is not "officially" part of the household – and is not registered as a resident – but usually sleeps in their house when Fernanda's son is home.

Fernanda is on the executive committee of her block's CDR and also the FMC, and is constantly writing documents, attending meetings or reporting to delegates from higher branches of official organizations. Although Fernanda is not a "true'" Tivolícero – as she was always quick to tell me, refusing to be seen as a source of "true" local history – everyone in the neighborhood knows her. Fernanda's enterprise and energy are not restricted to community work; in many ways these qualities seem to have defined her family's capacity to exist relatively comfortably. Although her household is not enviably well off, and they do not have close relatives abroad, the family is never short of food, and Fernanda says that they always have their basic needs met. Above the house, on the flat concrete roof, Fernanda raises pigs and chickens, slaughtering them periodically and selling some of the meat to neighbors, but keeping a substantial amount for the family. She also makes juice or soft drinks, either from fresh fruit and sugar or from packets of powdered mix bought in dollar shops, and sells the drinks at a peso a glass. Sometimes she sells cigarettes as well from family rations, and occasionally coffee, similarly obtained. The family does not have access to foreign or tourist-derived income, and the vast majority of family transactions are in Cuban pesos, of which they have a steady supply.

Fernanda is the sort of woman about whom revolutionary folklore is made. Although she recounted the struggles she had overcome, unlike almost everybody else, Fernanda never expressed to me any dissatisfaction with her material conditions. Her positive nature was a true testament to the revolutionary ideal of the worker's loyalty and generosity, and perhaps is a glimpse of a perspective fading from Cuban society. Her commitment to the revolution, and the social status this commitment confers, is not lessened (and is perhaps enabled) by her successful small-business activities, which seem antithetical to traditional socialist principles but are commonplace and publicly enacted in Cuba.

Elisabeth

Elisabeth grew up in the countryside, and her life is an exemplary case of the white rural family moving to urban Cuba due to changing work opportunities. Elisabeth moved to Santiago in her early 20s (she is now in her early 40s) with her husband, who works as a low-ranking official in the Ministry of the Interior. It is a respectable job, but provides too little salary for the family to live well. When I first met Elisabeth, she described herself as a housewife although she ran a manicure business from her house, which provided the money to buy most of the family's food and consumer goods such as toothpaste and laundry detergent. Elisabeth operates her business with her sister, and they allocate the profits between them according to need. They have a table set up with over 30 types of nail polish and a fluorescent light; they charge 10 Cuban pesos per manicure, and Elisabeth also offers artistic designs for a higher fee. Elisabeth explained to me that, although there are many other women who do nails within the area, she has a loyal clientele, partly because she often works on credit. As nobody has money all the time, she is very flexible about receiving payment at a later date; in return, she is able to buy other items or services from neighbors on credit when necessary.

Elisabeth considers herself lucky because most of her family still lives in the countryside near Santiago, and they come almost weekly to town with large supplies of fruit and vegetables for the household. Her food costs are therefore much lower than those of many neighbors. Elisabeth also usually keeps at least one pig in their internal patio, which she buys as a piglet and rears until adulthood to be slaughtered, eaten and sold. At the time of my fieldwork, Elisabeth's half-sister had recently married and left for Spain, and she had expected to send money and gifts several times a year. However, in the three years following her departure, she had not send Elisabeth cash remittances but instead items such as baby clothes, bras, perfume and souvenirs. At about the same time, Elisabeth got a job as a bathroom janitor in a local tourist venue, which allowed her to receive tips from foreigners of US$ 5 to US$10 a week, which has been a substantial help to her household.

In 2003 Elisabeth lived with her husband and two sons (one a teenager and one a baby), her sister and her sister's eight year-old son, and with an elderly woman to whom they are not related. The house in which Elisabeth's family lives was the woman's husband's home since the early 1900s, but because she had no children and her husband died over 10 years ago, she needed someone to care for her and the house. Elisabeth's husband made an arrangement with her so that he, Elisabeth and her son would move into the house and care for the old woman for the rest of her life. Later, Elisabeth's sister and nephew joined them. When the old woman died recently, they retained right of residence in the house, having lived there for over a decade. Both Elisabeth and the old woman, whom I knew briefly, spoke to me of their situation as mutually beneficial. But the prevalence of urban myths that circulate in Cuba about old people being cheated out of their houses, and the general disposition of most Cubans to gossip about their neighbors, makes it very likely that the arrival of Elisabeth's family in the Tivolí provoked much local comment and speculation. A cynical perspective on Elisabeth's family's motives as mercenary might be encouraged because the house is beautiful and spacious. Elisabeth's home is a double-fronted building from the colonial period in good condition as it is elevated from the street and sits at the top of the ridge that forms the Tivolí. The high ceilings, terracotta roof tiles and good ventilation make it a stark contrast to the stuffiness of many of her neighbors' smaller houses. The arrangement was made some time ago and is now very comfortably established. As her business attests, Elisabeth gets along well with her neighbors. Although she told me that the house belonged to the elderly woman, Elisabeth seemed to be in charge of the household; it was she who was always ready to receive visitors, who prepared the food, who allowed her baby to dribble cheerfully on the antique furniture and who worked with her sister giving manicures in the living room.

Reina

Reina is in her mid-30s, but looks 20-something; she is slim, white and attractive, soft-spoken and articulate. When I first met Reina, her household comprised herself (she identified herself as a housewife), her 11 year-old son who was at school, her common-law husband (unemployed) and her father and grandmother, both of whom received pensions. Reina's household did not include anyone with access to the dollar economy or even to a full-time peso salary. During my fieldwork, Reina worked intermittently for a local government initiative, which improved her income, but also increased her stress level considerably as no one was at home to care for her grandmother with dementia. According to a neighbor, Reina's father's pension was relatively good (122 pesos monthly, or US $4.90), but he was an alcoholic and drinks more than he receives. In the past, Reina's partner worked sporadically, and when working in a factory sometimes had access to products he could sell on the black market or that Reina could use herself. Reina has two other children who live with other family members – Reina is simply unable to support these two older children, although she assists whenever possible. For example, at the beginning of the school year Reina was very worried about finding a backpack for her daughter; it fell to her to pay for these larger items.

Reina's home was one of several at the back and side of a large colonial house, and one enters through a gate. Her small house was on one floor; consisting of a living room, a tiny kitchen and bathroom and two bedrooms. Although officially she had rarely worked, Reina gave me examples of strategies she developed over the years to support herself and her children. Reina says she is not ashamed to do whatever is necessary to get by: when her first child was born, Reina was a teenager and had left high school, so she made caramels to sell to neighbors. In the economic crisis of the early 1990s soap and detergent suddenly disappeared, and in Santiago people resorted to using leaves from plants growing in the countryside that when mixed with water had antiseptic and stain-removing effects. However the plants were unpleasant to touch, many people developed allergic reactions or rashes and the wash water would stain the women's hands. Reina took in the laundry of better-off neighbors for a fee, and this provided her major income during the most difficult economic period of modern Cuban history.[15]

More recently, Reina has sold to neighbors some food products acquired by her partner. But when necessary, Reina has also supplemented her income with informal sex work; as she explained, "If I need to find money then I will dress up and go out on the streets to find it," or "If I have to open my legs to feed my children, I do it without a problem." She does not have a regular clientele, nor does she identify as a sex worker, but rather charges men for sex if the opportunity arises and she is in need of money. She categorizes this as simply a marginally less acceptable way of using her body than washing laundry or making sweets. About a year ago, Reina met an Italian tourist who spent several weeks in Santiago over two visits. They developed a relationship and Reina was his girlfriend during his stays. In addition to enjoying the activities they could do together, Reina acquired several sets of clothing – bought in dollar shops in Cuba - and shoes, items for her children and cash

---

[15] Some neighbors were able to pay Reina because between1993-1995 many Cubans still had money; the problem was that there was nothing to buy, and black market prices for commodities skyrocketed. Services such as Reina performed would have been very affordable, but the "better-off" neighbors would not have been rich or even sufficiently fed during this time.

as a result of this relationship. Reina is very careful with the clothes acquired during this time, as they are her only "good" clothes, which she wears for going out and for work at her local government job. At the time of the Italian tourist, Reina did not have her current partner, and although she said to me that she hopes the Italian returns to Santiago soon because she needs the material help he can give her, she also indicated that she is now in a committed relationship and cannot or does not have sex with people other than her partner. She once told me that "a woman really has to be in love" to put up with having a husband, because he is a lot of extra work and stops you from other opportunities. I thought she was joking and began to smile conspiratorially until I realized that she had made the statement without any intention of irony.

During our conversations, Reina had told me that she desperately hoped to find a way to move out of her small house in the future so that she and her father could live separately. So I was pleased when several years later I went looking for Reina and was told by a neighbor that she had moved to the other side of town a few months before. Her grandmother had passed away, and she and her father had managed to swap their small house in the Tivolí for two even smaller apartments on the outskirts of town, but separate nonetheless.

Nilda

Nilda is a white woman in her early 50s who has lived in the same house in the Tivolí since childhood. When she married in her 20s, Nilda's husband moved into the house she shared with her parents, and they raised their two children there. Nilda separated from her husband approximately eight years ago and now lives in the house, significantly renovated over the years, with her two grown children, Nicolás, a student, and Sonia, an engineer. During my fieldwork Sonia married and her husband also came to live in the house.

As Nilda has lived in the neighborhood for a long time, she knows all of her neighbors and is well respected by people in the area. When poorer neighbors need some extra sugar, or an aspirin, they often ask Nilda to help them out, and Nilda is often called upon as a sympathetic ear and a mediating voice in disputes between neighbors or even between members of a family who have lived next door for many years. Although she is someone who has done well in her life, being a devoted daughter and mother, going to university, contributing to revolutionary campaigns in her youth and continuing to help neighbors, Nilda is well liked for her lack of pretension and her good treatment of everyone regardless of background.

Nilda works for a government institute in a professional capacity, earning a high salary by the scale of Cuban-peso incomes. Sonia and her husband also contribute some of their salaries to the household to buy food and other basic items. However, Nilda's job does not give her the time or connections to run a small business or to generate income in dollars, so until recently her household relied almost entirely on their salary for everyday spending. Despite her professional status and triple-income household, Nilda always had to budget very carefully to make sure she had enough money to buy groceries until the end of the month. She often told me that she was looking forward to her retirement, which she has since begun. Although she took her work seriously and was respected by her colleagues, she spoke of being tired of putting up with poor conditions in her workplace, of having to sit through long meetings, of walking long distances and traveling on crowded trucks to get to and from work and of not having time to take care of her house. Sonia helped Nilda in cleaning the house, but Nilda was responsible for all the grocery shopping and cooking for the family, which meant that as soon as she finished work for the day, Nilda would rush to the markets and the *bodega* (state ration shop) to buy food for dinner.

Nilda looked forward to retirement although her pension would be much less than her current salary because she felt that the salary in itself was not enough to justify making her life so troublesome. Fortunate circumstances are providing Nilda with more disposable income and material comforts in her retirement than she could have foreseen. Nilda has received occasional remittances from her brother in Miami; a couple of times a year he would send her $100. Her ex-husband also continued to contribute to the children's expenses. Although he did not give money to Nilda for food, he bought several high-cost items as he has a senior management role in an engineering enterprise. Nilda's ex-husband had bought the children a television, stereo and computer, as well as smaller items such as clothing and school supplies. Nilda's house was therefore one of the more comfortable homes I visited in the Tivolí. Then Sonia and her husband moved to Italy and almost immediately started sending regular remittances, which notably improved Nilda's standard of living. By 2009, her kitchen had a new microwave, and she had a mobile phone. Sonia's remittances were useful for daily expenses as well as major purchases. Nilda used them for groceries, no longer having to stretch out her use of expensive items such as cooking oil or shampoo.

Yanet

Yanet is a confident black woman in her mid-20s who lives with her mother and grandmother. She is a psychologist working at an institute in Santiago conducting psychological assessments and also making many home visits. Her mother worked in a pharmacy near their neighborhood, and her elderly grandmother was too old to do much housework, which was mostly managed by Yanet's mother. Since Yanet works full time and has no children, she does not take on the lion's share of the housework; her mother takes care of most shopping and cooking and uses all of her income on daily necessities. Although she gives her mother some money, much of Yanet's salary is used for transport, clothes, hair and nail maintenance and entertainment. When she isn't helping her mother with housework, Yanet spends most of her time hanging around with her cousins, or with young neighbors on a corner at the end of her street. Her boyfriend lived at the other end of the city so they did not spend much time together around her house, and unlike those of many of her peers, Yanet agreed that her relationship with him was not very close.

Yanet was on the executive committee of her local FMC. Her tasks involved attending fortnightly meetings on her block and helping to arrange events every few months. Although she did not consider herself particularly political, Yanet was a willing participant in FMC activities, and when it was relevant to our conversation spoke favorably about the achievements of the revolution in improving opportunities and creating equality for women. Yanet was generally proud of being "a Cuban woman," supporting the revolution and its achievements. Yet she openly criticized the shortcomings of the Special Period that had obliged her mother to struggle to provide good food for the household and to rebuild the house with years of economic sacrifice. She seemed to see her life and her mother's as an improvement on her grandmother's and the results of the hard-won success of both her mother and the revolution. One way she explained this slow steady improvement was with reference to their house. Yanet's house is built on what used to be a larger plot of land that was subdivided by members of her mother's family. Yanet's mother grew up in the house, and until the early 1980s it was a one-level cottage with a wooden roof. During that decade the house acquired a concrete roof and another level was added with two more bedrooms, a bathroom and a small sitting room in addition to the kitchen, bedroom and living room on the ground floor.

Yanet never had a relationship with her father, as he and her mother separated around the time of Yanet's birth. However, she knew approximately where her paternal relatives lived and also that her father had children by other women. As a teenager she came to know two of her half-brothers through mutual friends, and they subsequently developed a relationship and maintain contact. Both of these half-brothers are now in Europe. During my fieldwork Yanet was looking forward to the return of one brother for a holiday in Santiago; she had received two phone calls from him from Spain confirming his imminent arrival. She even hoped that one day she might follow her brothers to Spain. A year later, Yanet did actually move from her house in the Tivolí – to Havana, with her mother. They have returned to Santiago de Cuba for occasional visits, but I have not seen her since.

Dominga and Odalys

Dominga is a grand black woman in her late 80s who worked as a schoolteacher for many years before her retirement. Dominga moved to her house in the Tivolí approximately 60 years ago with her husband. Dominga's husband died quite young, and since then a woman whom Dominga considers her adoptive daughter, Odalys (now in her 50s), has lived with her. Although Dominga has blood relatives of her own – largely in the neighboring province of Guantánamo – her everyday support network and closest relationships involve Odalys's extended family.

Odalys's teenage granddaughter has also lived with them since infancy. The granddaughter's mother (Odalys's daughter) lives in the Tivolí as well, but in another house with her second husband, and they have a younger daughter together. Odalys's daughter and son-in-law eat their main meal every day at the house of Odalys and Dominga so that Odalys's daughter does not have the burden of cooking in addition to her full-time job. Odalys is in charge of the provisioning and cooking in her household, and she also does all the cooking for an elderly incapacitated neighbor, so she therefore cooks daily for six adults and one child even though only three people sleep in her house regularly.

Although I spent many hours with Dominga and Odalys, the fathers of Odalys's children and grandchildren have never been mentioned. For a long time, it never occurred to me to ask about them, as single motherhood seemed so utterly normal in the Tivolí. Odalys seemed always to have raised children without men around, and although she identifies as a housewife and has never worked in an official capacity, she has spent much of her life helping other single mothers raise their children. Her second, younger granddaughter is also in the house for an average of five hours a day as Odalys's daughter works after the operating hours of the childcare center. The little girl eats more often with her grandmother than in her official residence, and often stays overnight in her grandmother's bed.

Money for food is rarely a problem for Odalys because her two working daughters assist her economically; her second daughter lives in Havana and is married to a man from Germany. Among other things, she has purchased for Odalys a refrigerator, television, wooden living room chairs, a blender and a video recorder. This daughter is also able to send clothes regularly for various family members and sends money sometimes, although her contribution is more typically in the form of material goods. The Tivolí-based daughter provides more assistance with the daily living costs. As well as contributing their own rations and buying or acquiring food that is added to Odalys's rations for the group, she also gives Odalys money for her own needs and those of her daughter.

Although Dominga spends most of her time at home, much of her social sphere in the Tivolí is the result of her past professional and ongoing community work, first in the schools where she taught for many years and then in the local and municipal branches of the grandparents' circle, trade union organizations for retired workers and local cultural organizations. At the other end of the age spectrum, Odalys's teenage granddaughter does very little housework and is encouraged to work hard at her studies and extracurricular activities, including piano lessons, and the *Unión de Jóvenes Comunistas* (the Young Communists' Union) or UJC and an active social life, going out at night with friends and her boyfriend.[16] Within this family network of Odalys, her daughters and their families and Dominga, Odalys is the pillar of domesticity that allows the other family members to operate beyond the domestic sphere. As each year passes, Dominga's health has failed noticeably, requiring more constant care from Odalys and preventing Dominga from the social activities through

---

[16] All students, from pre-school to fourth-year high school, are known as *pioneros* or pioneers and belong to the *UJC,* which has corresponding organizations for secondary school and university students. In addition to attending school, children take part in extracurricular activity circles that they choose according to their interests and are also expected to attend events of political importance, such as festivals and May Day marches.

through which I had first met her. Odalys and other neighbors regularly say, "She isn't like she used to be," shaking their heads, in itself a form of recognition that Dominga has been a powerful figure in her local community, who in her old age commands a great deal of respect.

Tomasito

Tomasito lives with his wife and eight year-old daughter in what used to be one eighth of a nineteenth-century bourgeois house. It is tall and narrow, with a living room and kitchen area downstairs and a bedroom above on a homemade mezzanine level. Tomasito is lean, fit and is described by his friends as *mulato* (mixed) more often than *negro* (black).

The two qualities for which Tomasito is widely known are his humility and his hard work. During the day, he is a construction worker on government projects. However, this job provides less than 200 pesos (US$ 8) a month, which is not enough for him to support his family. Furthermore, there is not enough work to go around; workers have been sent home for months and received partial pay until another project came along. During these months they also missed out on the lunches provided, which were an important benefit of working. So to supplement his family income, Tomasito also works on the informal market as a painter and handyman. His prices depend on the economic situation of the client; if they have little, he charges less, and if they are better off, he charges a bit more. However, even with clients in better economic circumstances, Tomasito is known for charging very low rates for his labor, asking for as little as 20 pesos (less than 10 cents) for a few hours of painting.[17] Tomasito's services are in high demand in the neighborhood. Almost every day someone has a job they want him to do, and occasionally he has more work than he can manage, offending one client because he has been held up finishing another's project.

As Tomasito doesn't have a phone (few of his clients have phones either), all work arrangements are made face-to-face. In order to hire Tomasito to paint the walls of a house, an individual would go to his house or send word for him to visit the individual to discuss the job. He would then come to your house to look at the wall and discuss what you wanted done. Tomasito would then return on an agreed day and an approximate time (such as "in the afternoon") to do the job, and the fee would not be discussed until the end, when Tomasito asks the client to pay *"lo que quiera,"* (whatever you want), avoiding the indelicate task of naming a specific fee. It is up to his clients to know how much is appropriate to pay him, and as most of them have known Tomasito for years there is an unspoken agreement to be fair as part of friendship. Some wealthier clients give him used clothes, gifts for his daughter or give him advice

---

[17] This example highlights the gulf between typical official salaries and informal market labor rates even within the Cuban-peso economy in transactions between locals; an acceptable 200-peso monthly salary for a laborer would average to a daily rate of around 9 Cuban pesos for, theoretically, a whole day's work, plus lunch and some other benefits. In contrast, a whole day's labor for another Cuban working unofficially would rarely be less than 50 pesos, and would often include lunch as well.

or support in the form of a recommendation to a doctor, lending items for work or home or including him in their major family events.

Tomasito's wife makes small contributions to the family's income, sometimes selling biscuits and sweets from their doorstep on the street. She is not able to work more due to a neurological condition that led to a medical crisis, which created great economic problems in the household as money had to be found for medicine.[18] Tomasito was one of only two people I worked with who did not have a refrigerator, and he identified this as the domestic item that he needed most. Earlier he had saved to buy a gas range, which was the standard cooking appliance in Santiago de Cuba until 2006 when the Cuban government installed electric ranges.[19] Managing to purchase the new appliance seemed to have been quite an achievement for Tomasito, so

---

[18] The much-vaunted Cuban medical system, which is seen as perhaps the greatest achievement of the revolution, remains functional but has been susceptible to the effects of scarcity and shortage in the post-Soviet era. Although medical services are free and medicines almost free, pharmacy stocks are extremely low and very unreliable. Thus, one may need to rely on personal contacts to obtain scarcer medications which are officially available in pesos, or alternatively buy medicines which are only sold in dollars at "International Pharmacies" at first-world unsubsidized prices. The costs Tomasito mentioned in regard to his wife's illness were likely for scarce drugs through these paths, not consultations or hospitalization.

[19] From the mid 1990s until the government distribution of electric cookers in 2006 (see Chapter 4), most people in Santiago had gas stoves and tanks of cooking gas supplied by the government every 21 days. This method is safer and more efficient than the kerosene cookers used previously, which Tomasito's wife had been using. Oven cooking is virtually unheard of in Santiago; even people who actually have an oven almost never use it as it consumes too much gas.

saving up for a refrigerator, which would cost at least $300, might seem an impossible goal.

Apart from working and caring for his family, Tomasito's main interest in life is the *conga.* Tomasito plays the *tambor* drum, which he inherited from his family, and he grew up with the *conga* as part of his life. He is representative of the many people in Santiago who are not professional performers but ordinary men and women who, for a few months of the year, take part in their community's *conga* and Carnival activities. I was struck by the thought that Tomasito seemed to contradict the stereotypical image of a *conga* participant, perhaps *the* dominant image of Santiago masculinity and blackness: raucous, a hard drinker, not hard-working and living only for the crazy, fun moments in life (i.e. Carnival). In contrast, Tomasito is extremely soft-spoken, a dedicated family man who will happily *conga* for 12 hours straight but shows little interest in the violence, aggressive drinking and outrageousness for which the *conga* is usually known.

In the months leading up to Carnival,[20] beginning around May, Tomasito attends weekly rehearsals with the *conga* chapter known as *Paso Franco,* which is traditionally associated with the Tivolí and the street known as *Trocha* – two zones central in Carnival celebration. There are specific dates on which the *conga* takes to the streets, the

---

[20] In Santiago de Cuba, Carnival is officially 7 to 10 days culminating in the three most important days of celebration; the 25th, 26th and 27th of July (the 25th is the day of St James the Apostle/Santiago Apóstle, the 26th the day of St Anne/Santa Ana). However, the broader Carnival season begins on the day of St John/San Juan on 24th June, which is the special date for the Paso Franco *conga* to take to the streets.

musicians surrounded and followed by shuffling, dancing residents along well-known routes. Many *conga* participants also form the bands for *comparsas;* music and dance troupes that compete against those of other neighborhoods during each night of Carnival. Participants are not paid for the *comparsa* competition, although each participant is given a pair of tennis shoes in which to perform, and modest amounts of fabric are also provided by the Ministry of Culture to make costumes. Until the early 1990s participants were given clothes, enough fabric for elaborate costumes, food and refreshments. However, Tomasito told me that after Carnival 2,000 members complained because t-shirts were not available for each band member, although the tennis shoes continued to be distributed (and were often worn by his wife).

Tomasito's social and economic network is largely within the neighborhood, which is interesting given that he did not grow up around the Tivolí and only moved there in the late 1980s to share a subdivided house with his uncle. That he is not a native Tivolicero is overshadowed by the fact that most aspects of his daily existence revolve around local activities – almost all of his clients live within the neighborhood, his daughter's school and all of her friends are nearby, his wife's routine is based around the home and local amenities and his own leisure is entirely situated within the Tivolí through informal activities such as drinking on the doorstep and organized activities such as the *conga*. For Tomasito, the cost, transportation and sheer inconvenience of operating beyond the neighborhood is prohibitive; when the locally infamous leader of Santiago's best-known *conga* asked him to join his association, he declined not because of particular loyalty to his own neighborhood, but because it was too difficult to cross town with his drum every week and juggle his daughter's activities as well.

Dora

Dora is a black woman in her 80s who can claim to be a true Tivolicero; in 1887 her grandfather bought the land and built the house in which Dora still lives. Dora's grandparents were already residents in the area, working for the wealthy family that built and lived in what later became the Santiago police quarters and is now an important museum. Her father was a mechanic who spent many years working in Venezuela, and she attended a teacher-training college in pre-revolutionary Cuba. By the 1960s she was working as a local schoolteacher and, along with most Cubans of her generation, took part in many revolutionary campaigns, increasing literacy levels and transforming the education system. Retired for many years, Dora still takes part enthusiastically in a range of local civic/revolutionary activities; she belongs to the local *círculo de abuelos* (grandparents' circle), attends monthly meetings of the local association for retired teachers and is often invited to local cultural events.

Dora's house is registered in her and her three siblings' names. Living permanently in this house were 17 other family members, of whom 12 were registered as residents, including Dora, her husband, her three siblings and their partners, the siblings' adult children, partners and children and a couple of cousins and second cousins. Such a large number of inhabitants are not common in the Tivolí, but the house is very large, with eight bedrooms, an internal patio and two entrances.[21] Dora is very proud of her house, and I was originally introduced to her because her neighbors knew that she would enjoy sharing her family history and the history of her house with me. It was quite an impressive abode; the main entrance opened directly from the street into a large double-fronted living room. One wall of this room had a sliding door, which extended the width of the room for dinner parties and dancing. After the revolution, her siblings sealed the wall to create extra space for bedrooms. Despite the size of the house, people share beds or sleep in temporary spaces. The older generation are all retired and receive modest pensions of around 100 Cuban pesos (US $4) a month, while few of the adults of working age bring in a stable income. Dora describes her adult nieces as "housewives" and her adult nephews as doing "little jobs" or "getting things" *(él saca sus cosas)*. Such descriptions are deliberately vague and can refer to a wide range of informal income-generating practices. A complex pattern of domestic chores exists in the household, with each subsection of the family unit operating essentially independently; the unfortunate consequence for childless Dora is that, amidst the crowds in her lifelong home, she must largely look after herself. Her husband died several years ago and since that time Dora's own health has been failing. Family members only sometimes cook for her, and she does all her personal chores such as cleaning her room

---

[21] Dora reported several years ago that the house is 8.41 metres wide and 27.25 metres long.

and caring for her clothes. In Dora's household, her nieces and nephews need not care for her in order to justify their residence in the house, and they are also occupied with caring for their own parents and children. With no access to dollars or even extra pesos, Dora must rely on her rations and her pension to cover all of her needs, which is hard to do without hunger or some degree of personal neglect. Dora's circle of friends often supports her by having her eat meals with them, and bringing her with them to local social events or community activities. Dora is very respected by her peers and neighbors, but this respect is mixed with sympathy for her situation. Through her family's standing in the community, and her own education and professional career, Dora was something of a pioneer for black women of her generation, but despite working all her life, she has suffered unexpected hardship in her old age.

When I first met Dora, her impressive house still bore its original roof, although the paintwork on the exterior of her house had flaked off and several walls showed cracks in the brickwork. Dora had assured me that representatives from the urban planning department had been to examine the house and would soon begin repairs, as the tilework on the roof was falling off and leaks were creating further structural damage with each new hurricane season. When I returned to the Tivolí after a couple of years, Dora invited me in as usual to sit in the front living room and catch up on her news, but of the promised repairs there was still nothing to update. On a later visit, as on previous visits, I knocked at Dora's door in search of her, but something seemed different. As soon as someone opened the door, I realized what it was: the roof had completely disappeared, and the front section of the house was merely a façade with the living room a rubble-filled space into which sunlight streamed. Dora emerged from the remaining back section of the compound, and was pleased to see me. With no living room left in which to receive me, she brought me to stand in a corner where two remaining walls created a few inches of shade, and graciously asked after my family. Dora told me that a few months earlier her roof had finally been recognized as in imminent danger of collapse, and government representatives had come to demolish it. The walls remained while Dora waited for them to return and hoped for a new roof in the near future. Dora wasn't complaining; she was actually thankful that some action had been taken, and she was cheerful about the prospects of her precious house receiving some overdue attention. But – like her friends and neighbors – I couldn't help feeling sorry for Dora, so dignified, so accomplished, and yet so frail while her beautiful and beloved house slowly, steadily fell apart around her.

It is hard not to read Dora's relationship to her house as metaphor for the relationship of many of her generation to the Cuban revolution. But Dora herself is no metaphor, and my telling her story is not meant as an illustration of lost worlds or failed policies. It would be unfair to cite her story as the definitive morality tale in which Cuba is represented by decay without taking into account people like Nilda, Elisabeth and Yaima, whose lives have steadily, if not dramatically, improved. Along with the other individuals introduced here, Dora works through hardships in her life and adapts her daily routine to work around problems such as a missing roof. For me, Cuba is not to be found so much in a decaying house but in the people who continue to live there and in the practices that constitute what they describe as the "struggle" of getting by.

Chapter 2

Struggle and Other Key Concepts in Cuban Consumption

Luchar is a term invoked by Cubans in daily conversation; *luchar,* to struggle or battle, is generally used to refer to getting through life against the odds. Greeting a friend on the street, it is not uncommon to hear the response *"ya tu sabes; ahí, luchando"* ("you know; I'm here, battling"). *Luchar* is specifically used in reference to the struggle to obtain basic commodities such as cooking oil, vegetables or detergent, but can also describe other time-consuming activities to improve the life of an individual or family such as making a small profit in a business transaction, or securing a visa to travel abroad.[22] What characterizes a process or activity as *luchar* is generally that the tasks are difficult and time-consuming and that the outcome is unpredictable. *Luchar* is one of several verbs that rose to prominence in Cuban vocabulary in the early 1990s and

---

[22] *Luchar* can also be used in contexts unrelated to economic survival. For example, troublesome children give their mother struggle *("los niños están dando lucha a su madre"),* and university students struggle with their coursework (*"estoy luchando con la tarea de matemática"*).

describes the practices of everyday life since the Special Period, most frequently in reference to the search for scarce commodities. This chapter explores some of the ways in which the concept of struggle has been used by Cubans and how *luchar* has come to be a powerful concept in contemporary Cuba. Through the vocabulary that emerged in the Special Period– including *inventar* (inventing), *conseguir* (acquiring goods) and *resolver* (resolving problems) – I consider how the discourse of struggle is used to express dissatisfaction or anxiety while retaining a sense of humor and irony. Understanding the conversational forms of *luchar* prepares the reader for themes taken up more fully in Chapters 3 and 4. Understanding *luchar* also entails understanding the practices and objects through which everyday struggle in Cuba is materialized. Particularly for women, struggle is most often materialized through running a household and struggling to obtain domestic goods.

Litanies of Struggle

Discussions of life as struggle often take the form of a litany, which is a standard style of small talk among women in particular. Talking about how life is hard is a routine of daily interaction in Cuba. In response to various tales about the difficulties, frustrations or boredom involved, many a Tivolí resident will shake her head and agree wistfully that "it's not easy"; *no es fácil.* [23] Indeed, the most effective research technique throughout my fieldwork emerged from my earliest attempts to adopt such typically Cuban conversational styles. Absolutely the easiest way to engage a Cuban woman in conversation is to start talking about what is for sale (or more likely what isn't) in the markets, or to ask about when the water arrived or how long a power outage lasted. Such conversational starting points are taken as invitations to launch into a practiced litany of the frustrations of her day, her week or her lifetime. When women talk about the difficulties of daily life, the appropriate response is to sit and nod knowingly, adding "uh – huh" or "It's not easy," before sharing information about what I bought in the market, or how long it had been since my house got water. Such encounters, in which women talk about their latest problems using these particular narrative forms and standardized responses and gestures, are repeated every day in homes, offices, on street corners and in shops around the country. Events are almost always portrayed negatively, and unsuccessful ventures are depicted as frustrations and failures. Victories are presented as rare triumphs over odds so difficult that the acquisition is vested with the qualities of the sacrifice entailed in obtaining it. Such stories typically include a cast of surly bureaucrats, unhelpful shop staff, children outgrowing their clothes and empty-handed black market vendors. Crowded buses, empty

---

[23] This phrase is indeed so integral to the Cuban vocabulary that anthropologist Isabel Holgado Fernández uses it in the title of her study *¡No es fácil! Mujeres cubanas y la crisis revolucionaria* (2000).

marketplaces, houses without water and offices with broken air-conditioners are characteristic settings for the stories of small-scale frustrations that fill the conversations of women in Santiago. In addition to the particular phrases that lace conversations of this genre – ¡*no me digas!,¡oye eso!* and the inevitable ¡*no es fácil!* –such laments are generally accompanied by particular tones of voice and gestures. Raised eyebrows, pursed lips, rolling eyes and the slow emphatic shaking of heads seem to express that "Life shouldn't be like this, but we are too wise to dedicate any energy to fruitless outrage."

One example that shows how domestic life for women in Cuba becomes characterized as struggle revolves around the search for one of the most basic of goods in urban Cuba – eggs. Purchasing eggs in contemporary Cuba is a wonderful example of how acquiring even the most basic of items can require the exploitation of avenues and markets both legal and illegal, and how acquiring almost *anything* depends on extensive social networks. Eggs stand in an interesting no-man's-land of legality; they are sold openly by individual vendors, but are clearly illegally obtained and sold. Although people with chickens might conceivably have a small number of eggs to sell within the Tivolí, egg vendors walk through the neighborhood with precariously stacked trays of 50 eggs, selling them for a peso per egg. Such quantities of eggs can only be had with the help of the government granary, so selling eggs on the street is indisputable evidence of an illegal transaction. And yet, for the first months of my field research in the Tivolí, at least twice a day vendors would pass by shouting to all the world that they were selling eggs. This seemed to be an example of a tolerable illegal practice that was understood and overlooked.[24]

But suddenly there was an egg crisis. To celebrate my birthday, Nilda and I decided to order a cake made by a local woman who ran a small baking business from her home. With a few days notice, our neighbor would normally be able to acquire flour, eggs and sugar. However, although the week before vendors had passed with eggs every day, suddenly no eggs were to be found, both the extra eggs legally sold in the ration shops and the illegal eggs that street vendors touted almost daily had disappeared. Nilda mobilized her closest relatives to check in different shops and with their various contacts find enough eggs to make my birthday cake; three separate households combined their efforts for four days, and eventually eggs were found via a family member in another area of the city. As conversations regarding our egg quest took place on all the doorsteps of my block, it emerged that the previous week several people had been caught by the police unloading a truckload of black-market eggs just two blocks from where I was living. The people involved were arrested and, as they had evidently held the mother lode of eggs in our part of the city, no eggs were seen for months on the streets of the Tivolí. By the next month, I noticed that egg vendors had reemerged, once again selling industrial crates of eggs at 50 pesos a tray; the egg crisis had been resolved.

---

[24] The role of informal markets in grocery shopping is extensively addressed in Chapter 3.

The Daily Struggle for Consumption

When such experiences are repeated in each step in obtaining basic groceries for a household, it is clear why domestic economy is a topic of fraught consternation, tired fatalism or embittered outrage for women whose job it is to keep the house clean and the kitchen stocked. The efforts required and obstacles encountered by Cubans in acquiring goods for their households are such a frequent source of conversation and frustration that daily life is commonly thought of by Cubans as an ongoing and unpredictable struggle to manage daily consumption and family or household wellbeing. When asked what ideal or even reasonable levels of consumption would be, many of the people whose perspectives contributed to this study emphasized the contrast between what they felt their consumer experiences *should be* – providing enjoyment, displaying aesthetic appeal, and easing the burden of domestic life – and how consumption *actually is,* characterized by anxiety, unpredictability and struggle.

Struggle is the pathway to accumulation and fulfillment, whether spiritual, intellectual or material. Indeed, in Cuba and undoubtedly elsewhere, distinct categories of fulfillment (spiritual, intellectual and material) are rarely separable. This is clearly shown with the birthday-cake eggs: when Nilda's aunt called to say that she had found some eggs, Nilda put down the phone with triumphant emphasis and announced with pride that our problem had been resolved. Clearly, she was happy that she made a successful material acquisition, but her pride could equally be due to fulfillment of her role as a good woman and "adoptive mother," being sufficiently well connected to do the impossible by seemingly producing eggs out of thin air. To use the appropriate Cuban phrase, Nilda "resolved" (*resolvió)* the situation.

Fig. 5 *A typical birthday cake*

We can see how the concept of *luchar* involves a sense of triumph against adversity and of gain. But just as important to the notion of *luchar* is absence and sacrifice. To *luchar* is also to maintain the dogged resilience to go on in the face of frustration; to utter "I am struggling" (*estoy luchando*) is to communicate in one verb the years-long efforts and defeats in small acts of life. For every triumphant acquisition by a Cuban consumer – such as buying enough eggs to make a birthday cake –many previous similar attempts to acquire goods have failed. In conversations, consumption is a recurring theme largely defined in terms of absence or loss; to talk about food is to talk about how little food one had and how hard it was to buy more, and similarly with clothing or furniture people largely defined their possessions as lacking, or as having required enormous sacrifice. The goods that people possess are imbued with the memories of all the other goods one *should have had,* and with the pain and sacrifice required to get them. Having goods is therefore bittersweet because the struggle to obtain them makes possession difficult to enjoy. When I returned to visit Nilda after a two-year absence from Cuba, I asked if she remembered my birthday party two years before. Foremost among her memories of the event was not only the food and good company, but also the stress and effort of finding those eggs to bake the birthday cake.

The Discourse of Struggle

In 2006, on the doorsteps and in the living rooms of women I happily re-met after a two-year absence, I would ask how things were going in general and about the progress in their lives. The responses of the women were almost invariably permeated with bitterness and negativity, as they told me that life was harder than it was two years ago. For example, this is what Dominga had to say when I asked, "And how are things, generally?"

> *Ay,* Anna, things are really difficult generally.
> Yes, things are very hard… the problem is there

are a lot of things [to pay], and look, in terms of pension, I was getting about 170 [pesos monthly]. Well, for me they raised it by 56 pesos, so now I'm getting 230, but then they raised everything, the electricity.... But yes, it is getting harder to live, because they're persecuting the people who sell things on the street. And so you know that if you were in your house before, and you needed things, you had the possibility that a man would come along and people would buy from him. But not now. So it's hard work for everybody, and we can't go to the market either. Because in the market there isn't anything.

Dominga's lament makes the connection between the harshness of life and the absence of goods for sale, whether through state markets or informal avenues. What women such as Dominga mean in characterizing life as hard is that their daily lives are something of a grind; that goods are scarce, prices are high and obstacles to a "good life" seemingly insurmountable. Practical examples of life getting harder included higher electricity bills, the disappearance of black market vendors, and a reduced variety of goods on the shelves of stores. In other words, when the women of the Tivolí talk of life being hard in contemporary Cuba, they most specifically mean that life makes it hard for them to be good housewives, good consumers and good women.

My conversations with Dominga and other women in the Tivolí on my return suggested that there was more to this discourse than meets the eye. At the heart of the women's complaints seemed to be something more than an economic argument or calculation of the cost of living. I felt that to understand how and why Cuban women characterize their lives as struggle, I should not necessarily accept their depictions of life as *very much harder* as a statement of objective fact. Is there a particular hold that this image of struggle has on the lives of the women I spoke with? My intention in this chapter is to understand this largely negative discourse regarding the quality of their everyday lives and explore the concept of struggle (*luchar*) in contemporary Cuba. In doing so I recognize the justifiable reasons for frustration with and resentment of everyday life in post-Soviet Cuba, but I also critically consider how talking about life as a struggle is not only a reflection of the difficult circumstances of the lives of contemporary Cuban women.

Latin America has a propensity to describe life as *una lucha* or, in the case of Brazil, *una luta* (cf. González de la Rocha 1995:17; Friedmann, Abers & Autler 1996; Whiteford 1974:169-70; Scheper-Hughes 1992:187-88). But few Latin American governments have been as effective as Cuba's in harnessing the imagery of struggle in communications with its people. If the term used for daily life referred to the Cuban revolution, then the revolution repaid the compliment. Many aspects of daily life and social organization are described with military metaphors. The Cuban revolution is not presented as a series of military encounters during 1953-1959, but rather as an ongoing project of social reform and advancement. Citizens are regularly exhorted in newspapers and political speeches to face the adversity of Special Period economic shortages with dignity, bravery and steadfastness. It is a practice of the state to use military metaphors to describe Cuban identity and to conflate national integrity and wellbeing with individual integrity and wellbeing. Political debate, civil society, economic activity and community life are consciously presented by state media, and experienced by citizens, as integrally interrelated. By the late 1960s, the entire population of Cuba was exhorted to contribute to the (unfulfilled) goal of producing 10 million tons of sugar in 1970; this national productivity campaign was presented in terms associated with guerrilla combat; cane-cutting teams were "brigades" (Pérez 2006:259). Soon after the declaration of the Special Period, government billboards in Havana exhorted passersby, "Nothing is impossible for those who *struggle"* (my italics, Pérez 2006: 303). Similarly, after the Elián González affair in 2000, the cultural and ideological development of Cuba – and the distribution of many important goods – were organized through a public campaign entitled the "Battle of Ideas" (*La Batalla de Ideas*), intended to promote an alternative vision of sociopolitical development to that of neoliberal capitalism. With each new phase of social and economic transformation that has swept Cuba since the revolution, calls for self-sacrifice in battle remain central to official and vernacular discourse (Settle 2007:54-7, 95-6).

A History of Struggle

The power of this verb *luchar* is reinforced by its historical use in Cuba. The term *la lucha* has roots in the Cuban independence struggle against Spain in the late nineteenth century, and in the twentieth century, it was adopted to characterize the movement against U.S. domination as well as corruption and oppression under Presidents Machado and Batista.[25] Indeed, Cuban *mambises*, who fought for their nation's independence during the Ten Years War (1868-1878) under Carlos Manuel de Céspedes, were adopted as role models for the later guerrilla movement that was to become the Cuban revolution. School curricula, television programs and historical monuments and texts produced in contemporary Cuba uphold the heroism of the *mambises* as earlier soldiers in the same struggle that culminated in the revolution of 1959. A central component of the narrative that shapes the public history of both the nineteenth-century *mambises* and the twentieth-century revolutionaries who claimed to take up their mantle is the improvisational tactics of guerrilla warfare, which allowed victory in the context of material adversity. For the *mambises*, and for Fidel Castro and his comrades, the struggle of guerrilla insurgency was by definition a struggle against the odds. To win battles, they were required to

---

[25] De la Torre, *La Lucha for Cuba: Religion and Politics on the Streets of Miami* (University of California, 2003), p. 30. For a synopsis of the Cuban struggles for independence from Spain and the United States in the nineteenth and early twentieth centuries, see L.E. Aguilar, "Cuba, c. 1860-1930", L. Bethell (Ed.), *Cuba: A Short History* (Cambridge, 1993), pp. 21-56.

make creative use of whatever resources were at hand; they thrived on the element of surprise, and were fueled by faith in their objectives despite the severe lack of material resources. In this sense, the legacy of valiant improvisation left by such military heroes is perhaps not entirely irrelevant to the more banal struggles of women such as Nilda when she embarked on a citywide search for eggs to make a birthday cake.

The relationship of residents of Santiago de Cuba to these historic struggles is not abstract. As their city sits in the eastern heartland that was the center of the nineteenth-century battles for independence and of the later build-up to the Cuban revolution, residents of communities such as the Tivolí are well aware that they inhabit the same spaces and places in which the national propensity for heroic struggle has been enacted. Many residents of the Tivolí – including a few of the elderly citizens who became involved in my research – were deeply committed to and involved in the *lucha* of the 1950s that supported the incipient revolution. Santiago's proximity to the Sierra Maestra Mountains, where Castro, Guevara and their comrades were based, inspired many citizen supporters to join a covert movement that transported money, medicine, arms, food, clothing and other supplies to the guerrillas. This citizen movement, known as *la lucha clandestina,* now has a museum dedicated to it in the heart of the Tivolí, not a minute's walk from the houses of Dominga and her neighbors, housed in a building that was the site of a famous uprising in November 1956 (Pérez 1993:85). The Museum of *La Lucha Clandestina* prominently displays the goods inventively deployed by heroic guerrillas in the mountains:

Fig. 6 *The Museum of la Lucha Clandestina*

Fig. 7 *Interior courtyard of the Museum la Lucha Clandestina*

homemade Molotov cocktails, medicines, bandages and broken spectacles are among the relics of heroism in the face of material scarcity.

Fig. 8 *A display of homemade and improvised goods in the Museum*

As the displays also meticulously chronicle, women had important roles in *la lucha clandestina*. In addition to burying their husbands and sons with funeral processions that became increasingly political protests, women were integral to this movement with their skills in domestic production, preparing food, knitting socks and sewing shirts; in short, making use of skills similar to those of their daughters and granddaughters in their contemporary struggles.

The material culture on display in the museum of *la lucha clandestina* is compelling evidence of the socialist legacy of struggle that influenced the concept of *luchar* as it is invoked in daily life in the households of the Tivolí. Drawing from such images of bravery in the face of adversity, in contemporary life as much as in earlier phases of Cuban socialism, state institutions – among them museums – produce messages that evoke the nation's revolutionary history, using *luchar* and other militaristic terms, urging citizens to continue fighting onward and upward for a better Cuba. This message was reinforced by Cuban mass media before the crisis of the 1990s; issues of Cuba's leading magazine, *Bohemia*, from the 1980s include public awareness campaigns about the need to *luchar* against a wide range of practical and moral problems, ranging from questions of national security to the perils of poor posture in the workplace. As the Special Period crisis emerged and peaked between 1991 and 1993, the pages of *Bohemia* captured very clearly the increased pressure on Cuban citizens to endure serious material shortages with dignity, bravery and steadfastness inspired by the revolutionary heroes on the *Sierra Maestra* mountainside. Urban residents were encouraged to grow their own food and raise livestock (*Bohemia* 1/01/93:68; 05/03/93:68; 26/03/93). Readers are advised through the "handy hints" columns to find creative solutions for the absence of such items as toothpaste, deodorant or cosmetics by turning to herbal remedies and other domestic inventions. The chirpy advice seemed to suggest that using local plants as alternatives to toothpaste or deodorant might be the result of happening to forget a grocery item rather than an ongoing nationwide shortage in consumer goods (*Bohemia* 18/03/94:61).

Thus, the image of the contemporary Cuban consumer as a gutsy warrior fighting against great odds is not only a vernacular image, but is reinforced by the state. The *lucha* of local quotidian struggles has been analyzed by Marisa Wilson as distinct from what is referred to as a "capitalised version of *Lucha,* which refers to the national moral economy," but distinguishing between these two levels of discourse also demonstrates their interrelatedness. It is precisely the references to an official discourse of *Lucha* that make the everyday complaints of life as *una lucha* so potent, as "such communicative tactics often reflect efforts to balance demoralizing realities on the one hand with moral norms to continue the national "struggle" of the Cuban revolution on the other" (2009:165). For party officials announcing the latest programs in the "Battle of Ideas," or for writers in *Bohemia* magazine addressing the difficulties endured by Cuban citizens in the wake of the Soviet collapse, such hardships are largely attributed to the hostile trade and monetary policies of the United States. However, for many residents of Santiago de Cuba, to describe one's life as a struggle is more frequently an ironic allusion to the fact that the daily practices of contemporary life are not those envisaged in the inspirational speeches of revolutionary heroes.

Locations of Struggle: Across the Americas and into the Home

The guerrillas of the Sierra Maestra who fought in the Cuban revolution are not the only group that claims to be the political descendents of the nineteenth-century *mambí* nationalists. In Miami, Florida, Cuban emigrants have engaged in their own struggle to build (or rebuild) the nation of Cuba. Miguel de la Torre, a scholar of religion and a Cuban American, has written about religious and political symbolism in the concept of struggle (*la lucha*): "Today the typical Exilic Cuban on the streets of [Miami's] Little Havana understands *la lucha* as the continuing struggle against Castro and all who are perceived to be his allies" (2003:30). In Miami, the nationalist symbolism of *la lucha* is linked to the traditions of Catholicism; Christian imagery is central to anti-Castro propaganda, and the Catholic church remains central to the organization of social and political activism in the Cuban American community.

Luchar is also a politico-religious concept in the writings of the Cuban American feminist liberation theologist Ada María Isasi-Diaz. Isasi-Diaz describes herself as a "Mujerista" activist-theologist whose feminism is grounded in the struggle of Latina women for justice and liberation (2004). Isasi-Diaz terms the theology developed from such experiences as *la lucha,* and notes that her childhood in Havana was central to the development of her theological concern with the everyday struggle (*lo cotidiano*) of oppressed Latina women. Her biographical writings as well as her religious philosophy highlight the connections between three components central to the concept of *luchar*: loving the Cuban nation, having faith in the Catholic church and honoring the Cuban woman as the warrior of everyday struggle.[26] Isasi-Diaz's call to *all* Latina women engaged in struggle alludes to the plethora of examples in the literature, history and anthropology of Latin America that recognize the gendered struggle of women with regard to livelihood, domestic production and consumption and the maintenance of morality and respectability in the home, the family and the community.[27]

The prevalence of struggle as an (often gendered) attitude to life across the American hemisphere does not dilute its specific understanding in contemporary Cuba as the struggle associated with post-Soviet life. As Spanish anthropologist Isabel Holgado Fernández observed, home and the family became the primary trenches of resistance for women in this struggle (Holgado Fernández 2000:131-173). Despite considerable legislative reform to improve gender equality, in Cuba as in many other societies, the daily and weekly tasks of small-scale household provisioning has remained "women's work." Cuban women are not unusual in assuming domestic responsibility, and the similarities between gender-role

---

[26] See Isasi-Diaz's autobiographical notes on her website, http://users.drew.edu/aisasidi/bioInfo.htm.

[27] cf. N. Scheper-Hughes, *Death Withough Weeping:The Violence of Everyday Life in Brazil* (University of California, 1992), C. Weil (ed.), *Lucha: The Struggles of Latin American Women* (Prisma Institute Minnesota Institute of Latin American Studies, 1988), J. Friedman, R. Abers & L. Autler (eds), *Emergences: Women's Struggles for Livelihoods in Latin America* (UCLA Latin America Center, 1996).

divisions in Cuba and other Latin American and Caribbean societies have largely not been diminished by the reforms of the Cuban revolution. Although particular aspects of women's lives (such as contraception and free education) differentiate the opportunities of Cuban women from those of others in the region, in the areas of household provisioning, raising children, and housekeeping, the Cuban revolution has largely reinforced, rather than challenged, these practices as the primary domain of women. The economic crisis, in diminishing the role of wage labor while increasing the effort required in maintaining a household, further deepened the practical, economic and symbolic role of the home for women in Cuba (Pertierra 2008). More than previously from the 1990s on, houses and households became spaces in which women were most obliged to spend time, through keeping up with managing a household in conditions of shortage, and with decreasing incentive to remain active in salaried labor. The house and household became re-signified for Cuban women in what I have described in detail elsewhere as a gendered process of re-localization.[28]

After 1990, the Federation of Cuban Women (FMC) assumed public leadership in encouraging women to invest *more* time in domestic labor to cope with the effects of the economic crisis. Eckstein reports that the FMC encouraged women to take on non-industrialized household tasks such

---

[28] This argument is expanded with reference to my research in the Tivolí as well as a fuller discussion of research on gender and domesticity in Latin America and the Caribbean, in the 2008 article "En Casa: Women and Households in Post-Soviet Cuba," *Journal of Latin American Studies,* vol. 40 (4): 743-768.

as soap and candle-making, while newspapers and magazines published household tips and menu advice for adverse circumstances (2003:113). In the popular media women were applauded for their resilience and resourcefulness in finding new ways to keep their families fed and clothed despite economic adversity. Women in the Tivolí regularly told me of the "inventions" (*inventos*) they devised during the mid-1990s to maximize all available food, at times learning to prepare entirely new kinds of food. Neighbors shared recipes for food prepared in previously inconceivable ways; a most famous example of Special Period cooking was the introduction of *fongo* plantains (previously regarded as fit only for pigs), with even the plantain skins softened and fried as "steaks." [29]

Of course, there are other forms of getting by that particularly rest upon women's work, which are not sanctioned by the state and are regarded with ambivalence by Cuban women. With the return of the tourist industry, the most controversial strategy employed by women to generate income has been sex work and relationships with foreign visitors in the hope of material benefit (Rundle 2001, Pearson 1997:690). For women who have engaged in

---

[29] Stories of the *fongo* plantain skin "steaks" were told to me independently by several women in Santiago as the example par excellence of the desperate creative lengths to which people resorted with their food in the mid-1990s. Although I was unable to find evidence in newspaper and magazine archives from the period, some residents recalled television programs and print columns advising on the properties of *fongo* and offering recipes for *fongo* "steaks." Holgado Fernández has also recorded an interview in which a recipe for "plantain mincement" (*picadillo de plátano verde*) was given as evidence of the hardships of the early 1990s (Holgado Fernández 200:63).

more or less organized forms of sex-for-money, such encounters have been a crucial determinant of their household's wellbeing and represent a rare chance to realize a future in or beyond Cuba in which daily life need not be such a struggle.[30]

Russian Litanies and Cuban Luchas

Describing how women talk about their lives, I use the terms litany and lament not only because they capture the emotion and frustration of the women's words, but also because these terms are used by anthropologist Nancy Ries to describe a similar genre of women's conversations in Russia during *perestroika*: "Litanies were those passages in conversation in which a speaker would enunciate a series of complaints, grievances, or worries about problems, troubles, afflictions, tribulations, or losses, and then often

---

[30] Although it is important to recognize the impact of the post-Soviet crisis on women in particular ways, my intention is not to try to measure whether or how gender subordination has been magnified or alleviated by the impact of the Special Period on the lives and practices of Cuban women. Such projects have been undertaken with specific reference to Cuban women, and numerous similar studies can be found in various analyses of the socialist and postsocialist world (cf. Smith & Padula 1996; Safa 1995; Pearson 1997; Molyneux 1996; Gal & Kligman 2000; Pine 2002). My own interest is rather more on how the practices that are created by a gendered orientation to household management are related to identity formation and conceptions of normality through the consumption of goods.

comment on these enumerations with a poignant rhetorical question" (Ries 1997:84).

As defined by Ries, litanies are fatalistic, sorrowful and pessimistic, talking about loss and focusing on the past. This genre of spoken language sits in opposition to "cant," *cant* which is authoritative discourse that is positive and enthusiastic about the future promulgated in state media or by state officials:

> Personal narratives served as the grounds for people to perceive and promote themselves (individually and collectively) as important, even when they lacked concrete power or status. This social power was gained through often subtle discursive inversions of the values, plans and representations of reality promulgated from above, from the realm of Communist authority (p. 19).

For Ries, appropriating the terms and images of socialist discourse in pessimistic and cynical everyday speech is a form of resistance, revealing the absurdities of the official view of Russia compared with the harsh reality of life on the streets. Similarly in Cuba, talking about life as a struggle can be intended as a small act of resistance to the authority of the socialist state. However, for those whose worldview is dominated by the culture and structures of socialism, the adoption of socialist rhetoric with terms such as *luchar* is not necessarily ironic. When women such as Dominga, whose litany I quoted earlier, complain about life in Cuba, they would be horrified if I understood this as an attempt to ridicule Fidel Castro or criticize socialism. I suggest that there is not necessarily an *inversion* of authoritative discourse, but rather a *conflation* of discourses that could be expected to be ideologically opposed.

The power of *luchar* to describe the struggle of consumption lies in its flexibility to simultaneously adopt and critique Cuban socialism. Party officials and publications recognize the difficulties endured by some Cuban citizens, attributing such hardships to hostile trade and monetary policies of the United States. But as I noted earlier, for most people in Santiago de Cuba, to describe life as a struggle is to make a wry commentary upon the transition that many citizens made from struggling *for* Cuban socialism to struggling *with* Cuban socialism (Del Real & Pertierra 2008). Such a statement implies, but does not require, a criticism of the government itself for perpetuating economic hardship.

The Humor of Struggle and la Doble Moral

That the predominant expression used to describe contemporary life expresses such ambivalence, and is so open to unspoken multiple meanings that it can be employed to express a generalized frustration, is indicative of much about Cuban society – not least the importance of wordplay and poetics as subtle tools for political and social commentary. Humor and irony are also important aspects of how Cubans describe and discuss their struggles. In her excellent analysis of ironic discussions relating to food shortages, Marisa Wilson argues that "language performances in Cuba such as jokes serve *both* as outlets for subversion, *and* as ways to reconcile the state's inability to secure general welfare with collective values that rest above individual experience" (2009:165). Jokes and ironic statements work at seemingly contradictory levels simultaneously, as "It is not a stark contrast between pro-revolutionary or anti-revolutionary, collectivism and individualism, the state and the house" (Wilson 2009: 175).

In a related analysis, Tanuma argues that "the use of irony in Cuban conversation is precisely a means of escaping the pro-socialism versus anti-socialism binary" (Tanuma 2007:6). Whether or not it is being invoked ironically, *luchar* as it is used to describe daily life in Cuba draws from a multifaceted configuration of historical, religious and political language use.[31] But, to follow from the discussions of irony developed by Wilson and Tanuma, it is clear that oppositions continue to be important in defining Cuban identity and politics. For residents of Cuba in many meaningful ways, socialism is still opposed to capitalism, nationalism is still opposed to imperialism,"there" (Cuba) is still opposed to "there" (Miami). However, it is equally clear to Cubans that the opposition between these ideas is no longer so clear: To be a good Cuban is to accept remittances from your Miami relatives, to be a socialist activist is to be the first in line for the distribution of new

---

[31] This reinforces a point made by various scholars of socialism and postsocialism – of which Ries is only one example – that Soviet culture never erased pre-existing cultures and histories, and even consciously mobilised them.

refrigerators and to be a respectable woman is not only to dutifully attend meetings of your neighborhood revolutionary committee, but also to dutifully visit the statue of the Virgin of Charity, an incarnation of the Afro Cuban deity Ochún.

People are highly aware of these contradictions, and the concept of *luchar* is powerful because it encompasses the variety of Cuba's coexisting and contradictory histories and ideologies. Cubans make sense of contradictions even in the practical matters of everyday life. While remaining publicly committed to their community and to the Cuban state, individuals engage privately in behavior that they regard as immoral or, at the very least, anti-communitarian. Heather Settle writes of Havana: "Under the circumstances, the tension between belief and survival resolved into a powerful conceptual dilemma that has not ceased to be central to the lives of Cubans today: the so-called *doble moral*, or double ethic" (Settle 2007:117, see also Wirtz 2004: 414). Common and morally defensible situations in which one can invoke the *doble moral* are those in which individuals engage in behavior that they recognize as morally dubious in order to achieve the higher moral duty of providing material goods for their family.

As a term of value in both official and vernacular discourse, examples in this chapter have demonstrated that to struggle can mean to look either forward or backward and to be optimistic or pessimistic. More interesting, to struggle can also mean to do all of these things at once – *luchar* is a concept that fits the everyday existence of Cuban citizens. To return to Ries's categories of Russian talk, it is clear that *luchar* is both litany and cant. Just as *luchar* conflates two opposing categories of discourse, the activities in the struggle of everyday life in Cuba require the flexible conflation of socialist and ostensibly anti-socialist activities. *Luchar* is such a powerful term because it expresses the schizoid components of politics and identity that co-exist in most Cubans' lives and minds; in other words, *luchar* is a concept that serves as a dignified counterpoint to the more uncomfortable existence of *la doble moral.* Not only can a woman's struggle to get food on the table be socialist, nationalist, post-socialist, anti-socialist, woman-centered or capitalist, but it is frequently many of those things at once! It is the co-existence of these factors, and the knowledge that their coexistence seems ridiculous, that invests one simple verb, *luchar,* with such richness and gravity and humor.

Inventions, Acquisitions, Resolutions: Describing the Special Period

In the early 1990s, a number of other verbs rose to prominence with *luchar* so that the words and their related practices constituted what Amelia Rosenberg Weinreb has described as a "Special Period Lexicon" (2007:109). Like *luchar,* these verbs were understood as referring to complex attitudes and practices that emerged from the specific material difficulties. A primary "weapon" in the Cuban struggle for consumption is the practice of "inventing" or *inventar.* The concept of *inventar* incorporates a variety of strategies that are improvised solutions to the practical problems presented by trying to be a consumer in Cuba. When women planning a special meal run out of gas to cook with, *hay que inventar* ("you have to invent") by obtaining an illegal second gas canister or by borrowing the kitchens of friends and neighbors. Houses being renovated are frequently a site of "invention," using the creative recycling of any possible building material and the improvisational handiwork of volunteer laborers and self-trained artisans. Young men and women with no steady income are often masters of inventing as they buy and sell items such as clothing, CDs or jewelry they have obtained through work contacts, foreign friends or random circumstance.

An important connotation of the verb *inventar* is that something appears to be produced from nothing; indeed, when most Cubans present the results of their inventive strategies, such as a new outfit, a renovated bathroom, or a birthday cake, they usually behave as if these products had been produced from thin air. People rarely explicitly describe the source of such goods; to openly discuss the illegal activities involved, the indignities suffered, or the savings hidden in order to procure new goods would be seen as poor taste in some contexts, and downright dangerous in others.

Another concept central to Cuban consumption practices is *conseguir,* which can be partially translated as "acquisition," although this definition alone is unsatisfactory. If the general state of life in Cuba is a battle, and if the response is to invent, then the victory at the end of this process is the acquisition of goods. Sometimes *conseguir* can mean shopping or buying, but more often is an acquisition that has involved no money – pilfering, swapping, borrowing or being given goods can be included as acts of *conseguir* (Rosendahl 1997:41-3). Making an item would not be described as *conseguir,* which confirms that this term refers to consumption and not production. Because acquiring goods is usually difficult, to describe something as having been acquired (*conseguido*) also implies obstacles and complications overcome along the way. For example, women may visit five or more shops around the city hunting for laundry detergent or looking for affordable sheets. If they are unsuccessful in their mission, they might ask an acquaintance traveling out of town to make such purchases on their behalf. If someone is planning a party, they use all their networks of contacts to get a good price for some black market alcohol, or to borrow a car to visit farmers selling pigs for roasting. Above all, the workplace is an important site for successful acquisition, with bakers acquiring cooking oil, fishermen acquiring fish, hotel staff acquiring lightbulbs and construction workers acquiring cement. All of these are included in the process of *conseguir,* and the triumph with which stories of successfully finding these goods are told is indicative of how apt the battle metaphor is for describing consumption in Cuba.[32] It is often through invention and

---

[32] Even tasks that would in other circumstances be seen as forms of production – such as rearing pigs and fishing – are in urban communities such as the Tivolí largely determined by the lack of other avenues for consumption, as the state mechanisms that were intended to reduce the need to struggle with everyday consumption have been

acquisition that Cubans manage to *resolver* the specific problems of shortages that defined 1990s Cuba (Settle 2007:35-6).

The rise of such concepts as *inventar, conseguir,* and *resolver* to describe everyday life generated new genres of popular culture that chronicled the changing times through music, writing and art that captured international attention. Frequently, problems related to consumption were at the fore of such cultural moments – as when the group Orishas sing of starting a new day "to struggle, to invent....have to get the beans cooking, there's no water left to wash." Geoff Baker notes that the deliberate ambiguity of *inventar* made it a key theme in Cuban hip-hop that captured the "complex realities of rappers' lives" (Baker 2006:228). In novels, Esther Whitfield suggests that *"resolver* and *inventar* overreached themselves as the verbs of the moment, becoming practices for survival whose structural proximity to artistic creation, or to making something of nothing, haunts the period's literature" (Whitfield 2008:3). In writing, rapping or singing about their struggles, artists were "inventing," artistically and economically, their way out of the problems of the Special Period with music festivals, tourist venues, literary competitions and international universities seeking the valuable creative resources of Cuban artists (Hernandez Reguant 2002).[33]

---

insufficient so as to oblige citizens to think about and work toward consumption more than ever.

[33] It is worth noting that the members of Orishas wrote the song quoted, "Bombo," after having lived in Europe for several years. The irony is not lost on Cuban artists that chronicling their difficulties can represent the best way to relative prosperity.

But the creativity of Special Period practices was not confined to the arts; in the 1990s, all Cubans became everyday producers of a new culture in which improvisation and ingenuity were key to economic survival. The difficulties lamented by the women in this chapter also propelled Cuban citizens to an "explosion of creative energy," (Settle 2007:36) as even in basic household provisioning, people became *"bricoleurs, creating new stuff out of given cultural material"* (Wilson 2009:176).

The Universality of Struggle

What makes the concept of struggling for consumption so relevant to the character of contemporary Cuban life is that all of the variables of Cuban identity seem to unite in it, the same way that all engage in this struggle regardless of their circumstances and opinions. My research included people who range from ardent socialist hardliners to cynical youths eager to leave the country, and without exception every person with whom I worked and lived characterized life in Cuba, and in particular consumption practices, as deeply problematic. The women who participated in this ethnography generally characterized their efforts to manage a household as embittering and exhausting, and in part these characterizations are a response to their continuous exposure to the romantic nationalist exhortations of struggle by politicians and the media. In private, typical responses to such romantic representations of Cuba's present struggle include cynicism, incredulity or sadness at the distance between official representations of revolutionary advancement and their daily experience. People expressed mixed emotions and perspectives about the reasons for Cuba's failure to provide them with satisfactory life opportunities, although some preferred not to discuss such ideas at all. Others were more explicitly critical of policies and ideologies they saw as responsible for material shortages since the 1990s. Nevertheless, for most Cubans, complaining about consumption in terms of struggle was alluring precisely because such discourse is not explicitly political; *everybody* complains about shortages and high prices in Cuba, and nobody can be blamed for doing so. To bemoan the absence of goods need not imply a defense or a critique of socialist planning policies, although in a society where political debate is difficult and political allegiances are fraught with tension, such implications are often made in the relatively safe sphere of discussing consumption. Whether as an outlet for broader frustrations or as a ritualized entrée into social interaction, talking about goods, and about the efforts required to acquire them, constitutes a significant part of daily conversation and occupies an even greater place in people's minds. For these reasons, such conversations were a wonderful starting point from which I began to understand individual behaviors of social reproduction in contemporary Cuba.

Chapter 3

Battling for Groceries: *Shopping, Stocking and Household Management*

One of the striking transformations that the economic crisis of the 1990s created in urban Cuba was the sudden scarcity of groceries. This chapter focuses on consumer goods related to food, because food products are cited by Cuban women as the most basic of "necessities" (*necesidades*). Some of the most necessary groceries, such as cooking oil and meat, can be expensive and inconsistently supplied via the multiple markets that shape food consumption in Santiago de Cuba. After outlining what is a rather unusual framework for grocery shopping, this chapter shows how difficulties encountered and strategies to acquire food commodities have become fundamental to women's sense of self and to their characterization of life in contemporary Cuba.

Acquiring food and groceries for a household is usually the responsibility of mature but not elderly women; typically household managers are between 35 and 65 years old and are mothers or grandmothers of a family unit. When men are involved in domestic maintenance and reproduction, they are more likely to be in charge of small businesses (such as rearing animals) and building projects such as repairs and renovations, but women are also found doing this work. During my research, although I met many men who expressed great enthusiasm for hearty Cuban food, and who took great pride in being well-groomed and wearing neatly laundered clothes, I did not know any who regularly cooked, laundered or cleaned house. Many men assisted their wives, mothers and daughters with shopping, but they were usually sent to obtain specific items rather than being regularly in charge of household consumption.

Accordingly the residents of the Tivolí who responded most enthusiastically and with the greatest detail to questions about domestic consumption were women, the domestic managers of their homes. Of the women profiled in Chapter One, four (Fernanda, Nilda, Elisabeth and Reina) were in charge of the shopping and cooking for their households. Relatively young women like Yanet, who relies on her mother to manage the house; elderly women like Dora, who looks after herself with some support from a larger household; and Dominga, who had passed the management of her domestic economy on to her adoptive daughter Odalys, usually had less to contribute to these discussions. Although Yanet, Dora and Dominga contributed to household spending and housework, none saw themselves as in charge of the household economy. But all three women engaged in the everyday conversations that understood the struggle of daily life for women as manifested in shopping, cooking and cleaning. The success of domestic activities is largely dependent upon the regular supply of consumer goods through public institutions, and many of these goods simply have not been consistently or affordably available.

Cubans frequently focus on food insecurity and lack of food variety as the worst aspects of post-Soviet life. This is especially so for women in charge of the household meals, whose task of creating appetizing, filling and "strong" meals is felt to have become especially challenging. A "strong" meal – *una comida fuerte* – should ideally consist of rice with beans (cooked together or separately), some kind of *vianda* (the broad category of root vegetables that also includes plantains), a salad of one or two types of seasonal vegetable and a serving of meat. In practice, meat may be replaced by eggs, or used more sparingly when cooked with the beans. Salad might easily be missing through seasonal or economic circumstances. As anthropologist Mona Rosendahl has noted, for Cubans having plentiful food is frequently associated with living a good life, and big plates of food including a large serving of meat are very positively valued. Cooking and serving strong meals is an important part of being a woman, and eating them with relish is an equally important part of being a man (Rosendahl 1997:36, 49-50). Of all the necessary components of a strong meal, meat is the most significant, and the quality of a meal is usually determined by the quality and quantity of meat served. As has been found elsewhere in the Americas, food in Cuba is understood to be the primary source of strength, and meat in particular is the "strongest" food available (cf. Orlove 1997:257; Scheper-Hughes 1993:158, Gudeman & Rivera 1990:28-9; Bentley 1998:91-102). The collective term often used for meat and fish is "protein" (*proteína*); this category however excludes other protein sources such as eggs, beans and soy products (Pearson 1997:683-4). Soy protein is particularly disparaged by Cubans; the subject of many a joke when served in workplace or student cafeterias. As a longstanding government-issued substitute for meat it has become symbolic of the very food insecurity of the 1990s that it was to assuage.

Although lunch and dinner are ideally both strong meals, in practice, people may rely on one homemade strong meal a day, whether at midday or in the evening. Students and workers may eat lunch at workplace cafeterias, while families at home during the day may prefer to eat a heavy lunch. In contrast, breakfast in Cuba is typically light, consisting of strong, sweet coffee and the daily bread-roll ration, which is delivered each night from the government-run bakery. Milk and dairy products are largely reserved for children and the elderly, and in Santiago de Cuba dairy supplies are poor.[34] Fruit and vegetables are in more plentiful supply, but are seasonal from local sources. Tomatoes, avocadoes and cucumbers are common vegetables, with shorter seasons of lettuce, cabbage, green beans and carrots appearing in the cooler months. Bananas and guavas are available virtually year round, and oranges, mangoes, tamarind and grapefruit arrive seasonally. Plantains and root vegetables, such as *malanga*, potato, sweet potato and cassava are frequently available, although rarely would all be available simultaneously. Typical snack foods often sold at street stalls include pizzas (flat bread

---

[34] In some other areas of Cuba, such as the province of Camagüey, where much of Cuba's dairy industry is based, milk is readily available most of the time.

cooked with tomato paste and cheese) or small sandwiches (bread rolls with a slice of cheese, ham or roast pork inside). Spaghetti with tomato sauce is another snack more frequently made at home and not really considered a strong meal. On the street one can also buy a range of homemade biscuits, peanuts, lollipops or pork rind snacks from individual vendors, but these items are not considered meal substitutes.

Other groceries are available for purchase in the dollar shops known as *la shopping* (such as cans of beer and soft drinks, packaged spaghetti, mayonnaise, pickled goods), but they are rare supplementary items for a fortunate few of the residents featured in this chapter; they do not form part of a regular basic shopping list. The range of food and drink outlined above can be considered a comprehensive account of what is available to residents of Santiago on a daily basis. Although the diversity of food may not be limited in absolute terms, in comparison to the food-shopping options available in other cities in Latin American and the Caribbean and, more important, in the opinion of the consumers themselves, options for food and drink seem extremely limited. Food security and food variety are remembered by residents of the Tivolí as having been better "before"; the tinned meats, preserved fruits and pickled vegetables imported from Eastern Europe in the Soviet years are remembered with nostalgia by all but the youngest people. Even in the early 1960s, U.S. brands including Quaker Oats, Philadelphia Cream Cheese and Coca-Cola were standard fixtures in the local Sears and Woolworths, and more generic food items including wheat, beans, rice, lard, poultry, eggs and dairy products were also imported from the United States (Benjamin, Collins & Scott 2003:349). Although in affluent capitalist societies, buying local food and reducing reliance on processed food may be seen as desirable, socially distinctive and environmentally sustainable, for Cuban shoppers it is seen as the necessary consequence of an enduring food and consumption crisis.

Negotiating Multiple Markets: Rations, Vendors, Markets and Dollar Stores

The easiest way to start a conversation with any household-managing woman in the Tivolí is to talk about what food can be found in local shops and markets. Sitting on rocking chairs in a woman's living room, sisters and neighbors chat at length about the rise in the price of vegetables. News spreads rapidly as basic goods arrive in the *bodega* (neighborhood rations shop), and women hurry to queue so as not to miss out.

For the more affluent, the arrival of processed foods such as tomato paste or mortadella in a dollar store is news worthy of a phone call and a special visit to the town center. Nobody knows exactly when food will arrive or for how long it will be available, and there is an acute sense that the battle to feed the household is a battle against forces beyond consumer control.

It may seem ironic that the clearest example of this sense of lacking control can be seen in the very part of food provision that is guaranteed: the state allocation of the core of a household's food supply. Each house in Cuba has a ration book listing quotas of goods for each resident.

Fig. 9 *The neighborhood rations shop*

However, the number of residents officially listed in a house is rarely an accurate reflection of the number of people regularly eating at the table. Dora's house was the most extreme example of this I found, as it regularly housed 17 members of the extended family, of whom 12 were listed in the ration book. In contrast, Nilda's household received more than their official portion, as Nilda's husband, long gone from the house, left his quota behind to help support his children. The rationing of basic foodstuffs has varied across the decades. For example, in the late 1960s rationed goods accounted for a majority of items consumed, but by the 1980s many consumers could afford a range of available goods in addition to their

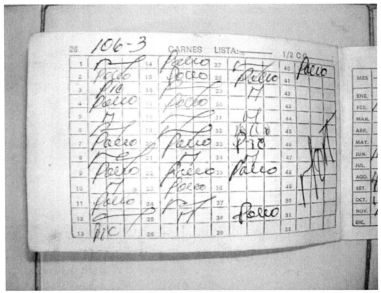

Fig.10 *Pages in a ration book*

rations.[35] After 2000, rationed goods typically accounted for around half of the average person's food intake. Although there is some variety in the rations issued each month, core items such as rice and sugar are always present. Other foods such as spaghetti are irregular features, and, although

---

[35] For example, Benjamin, Collins & Scott report that in 1983 export-quality rum appeared in shops at the expensive equivalent of five times the average daily wage (Benjamin, Collins & Scott 1986:41). By comparison, in 2004 a bottle of export-quality rum in a dollar shop would cost between US $4 and $10, or between 8 and 20 times an average daily wage. Whereas in 1983 a bottle of Spanish olive oil cost 20 Cuban pesos per litre (Benjamin, Collins & Scott 1986:41), by 2004 such bottles were prohibitively expensive (US $8 or 200 pesos) and even a large bottle of locally produced vegetable oil cost around US $2, or 50 pesos.

eggs arrived every month during my research in 2003-2004, the type and quantity of meat, fish or soy fluctuated from month to month.

During a recorded interview, Nilda outlined to me with remarkable precision the typical rations issued to four people for one month:

> This month, per capita: six pounds of rice, eight ounces of beans, five pounds of sugar, and salt. Right now they're distributing the salt tri-monthly because it already comes treated and it seems that they're also using it for export, so it comes in higher quality, but it comes every three months. This is what's arrived for the family rations this month...and coffee, which they give at four ounces per capita. Four ounces. That's what makes the basic family "hamper" [allotment]. And at the butcher's, in this month, they've given chicken, at 10 ounces per capita which is not the norm, usually they give 6 ounces – but this time they gave 10, and 6 eggs per person, which they just gave. That's what arrived at the butcher's this month. For the month. At least from 1 August until now [10 August]....Oh, I forgot to say that they give a half a pound of oil per capita per month. Half a pound per person monthly...for about the last year – because before that they didn't give any. And the rest of the oil, you have to buy on the black market, or with dollars, you have the two options. Weekly in this house, to cook for four people without running short – which is to say,

>having more or less normal food, not being able
>to fry large quantities of potatoes every day, just
>being normal – one liter of oil lasts at most eight
>days. Eight days, or nine if you're careful. Nine
>if you're careful. So most of the time, I have to
>buy around three liters extra outside the ration.

As Nilda is quick to suggest, the food issued via rationing is merely a starting point for feeding a household; products other than sugar, rice and beans frequently need to be supplemented by food acquired in other ways and at higher prices. For families without the means to buy quantities of meat and vegetables, even the basics of rice, beans and sugar can run out before the end of the month. Nilda almost always has leftover sugar late in the month that she gives to neighbors who run out, because the neighbors frequently replace a meal with sugar-water when they lack the means to buy a variety of food.

Special extra allocations or "diets" (*dietas*) are given on the basis of health, age or occupation. Young children are given milk and yogurt rations, and the elderly also receive extra rations. In Reina's house, her elderly grandmother and young son are both allocated supplemental rations in addition to the regular rations for herself and her father. Fernanda's household contains several members with diets for health reasons. She and her daughter have both been diagnosed as diabetic and receive extra quotas of chickpeas and root vegetables as a result, and her granddaughter, who was diagnosed with the autoimmune condition *lupus erythematosus*, also has extra allocations of chickpeas, root vegetables and dairy products recorded in her ration book. Some other rations are dependent upon occupation – for example, one neighbor assured me that fumigators receive a diet of food items to combat the dangers of the fumes inhaled in their job. Other goods are allocated to citizens according to age; 10 packets of cigarettes a month are still allotted to each adult who was born before 1955, although this policy does not apply to younger generations. Thus, older non-smokers such as Fernanda receive cigarettes while younger smokers such as Nilda's son-in-law do not. Fernanda sells her unused cigarettes to neighbors at a peso a piece, while Nilda's son-in-law goes through the monthly rations of both his non-smoking parents before he is obliged to buy his own.[36] Redistributions of such goods take place frequently within households for free, and between households for money. Despite the illegality of reselling rations, there is evidence that the practice of exchanging or bartering unused rations has been common since the earliest years of the system (Lewis, Lewis & Rigdon 1978: 91; Benjamin, Collins & Scott 1986: 43-46).

All the rationed goods mentioned must be collected from a designated shop; the *carnicería* (butcher) in the case of all

---

[36] In August 2010 cigarettes were removed from all rations as part of the continuing gradual process by which the rations for groceries has declined (for press coverage, see http://www.guardian.co.uk/world/2010/aug/26/cuba-cigarette-rations-cut). That the subsidy continued for so long, while many food items had long disappeared from ration books, is a testament to the cultural and economic role of smoking in Cuban culture. Cuba has one of the world's highest rate of smokers at nearly 40% of the population, and until 2008 tobacco exports earned Cuba around US $250 million a year, although since then tobacco cultivation has declined (World Health Organisation 2010:103; Economist Intelligence Unit 2008:40).

food that needs refrigeration, such as meat, fish and dairy products, and the *bodega* for all dry goods. In the Tivolí there are two *bodegas* and *carnicerías* from which most of the community collect their rations. Working women are given priority in the queue in recognition of the hours they sometimes wait for products to be unloaded and allocated. Each person in the queue has the household ration book in hand, and the goods they collect are marked off by the shop attendant. On occasion these shops are sent more goods than rations require, and the extra goods are sold "above price" at non-subsidized prices. Such events are not reliable, but when available seem to be a preferred option to the black market, although the goods may in fact be exactly the same; in the Tivolí, the sources of various black market foods are usually employees in local shops or bakeries. Reina's household, and that of her neighbor Yanet, show two aspects of this distribution of goods from shop to household by rations and other means.

> *Reina:* Um, my grandmother can't miss her *malanga* or pumpkin or *fongo* plantains, because that's what she eats pureed, because she's sick. She can't eat rice or anything like that anymore. Sometimes I buy fish "above price," a little piece of meat, that's what I mostly buy, apart from the quota.

> *Anna:* Do you buy extra cooking oil?

> *Reina:* Well, at the moment, no. Because the partner I have right now, he's working in a bakery, so he gets a little oil, you know. So it's very rare moments that I'd be buying oil. At home sometimes we buy lamb or whatever, but

it's just a little piece, a pound or less – we can't buy more. Anyway I don't really have that taste. We don't buy eggs in the house. At the butcher's we do when it arrives.

Yanet's Mother: One example. You buy [vegetable] oil…right there in the shop. If not, it comes from there anyway; what they sell in the street comes from the shop, or someone from the shop gives it to that person who sells it to me. So this oil comes from the shop; almost always, so you know where it's coming from.

Nilda: The bread arrives almost every day. One bread-roll per person which has a set quantity, a set weight that it should have, a particular size of roll that should have a set number of grams that I can't remember right now. But it never has that weight because they steal. Because with the weight they steal, they make 100 more rolls and earn 100 pesos. So the bread they give you that you eat is never the bread that you're allocated. It should still be a bread-roll, but a better roll, and a bigger one.

Thus, basic foods that arrive via the rationing system can be acquired in a variety of ways. Rationed goods can be purchased legally according to the allocations in the household ration book, and can also at times be purchased legally above price at the ration shop. Other goods sold above price are illegal sales, as for example in the case of bread-rolls, which sell for a peso per piece. Finally, rationed goods that have been siphoned off by employees before the point of sale supplement family diets or are sold at low prices on the neighborhood black market. Even in this basic food supply and distribution, the spectrum of legal, illegal and semi-legal transactions confuses the boundaries between the official, black and grey markets. People involved in such transactions, whether buyers or sellers, can be unsure as to just how legal or illegal their activity is, as laws pertaining to private sales have changed many times and distinctions between "giving" and "selling" or between "personal use" and "resale" can be difficult to ascertain (Benjamin, Collins & Scott 1986:44-46). Openness and covertness combine in the distribution of goods in which everyone relies on technically illegal undertakings that are only obliquely acknowledged.

Vendors and Markets

In years past, the bulk of the Cuban daily diet was supplied by the state. However, in the most difficult years following the Soviet collapse, the government legalized around 300 small business ventures, including the selling of food to supplement the much-decreased government rations issued to citizens. The return of ambulatory vendors – called *pregoneros* and a trademark of Santiago daily life – was, according to Nilda and Dominga, almost immediate, and the practices and styles of individual selling almost reproduced pre-revolutionary customs (Barnet 2004).

In Santiago de Cuba, each vendor has a standard repertoire of goods for sale, and walks the same route at roughly the same time each day. The approach is advertised by an individual song or call that describes what is for sale in a unique manner. Thus, residents' daily routines are punctuated by the soundscape of passing vendors, whose presence is a part of neighborhood life and for whom longstanding customers will wait to purchase specific items. Early morning items for sale tend to be bread and some fruits, no doubt useful at breakfast. ("Oranges! Sweet oranges, oranges! Sweet oranges!") [37] As morning progresses, a range of fruit and vegetables pass; the schedule seems to be determined by the opening of the central market from which much produce originates. ("There's avocado there's onion there's pepper, the go-od pu-ump-kin!")[38] In early afternoon the intensity of the sun generally discourages selling or indeed any other street-based activity, but by around four p.m. a second shift of vendors emerges, selling snacks and ice-cream and bread to fill a pre-dinner space and capitalize on the after-work hours when almost everyone is at home. ("The 40-cent biscuit-man has arrived! Neighbors, I'm going! I'm going! The 40 cent biscuit-man!") [39] By nightfall business is done, and the only neighborhood options for buying food are the housefront stalls selling pizzas and snacks. There are more vendors in areas such as the Tivolí than in other parts of the city. The population density and proximity to central markets offer a shorter day's work for the vendors, who either come to town daily from outlying areas, or buy goods at the town markets and work their way outward until they sell their goods. Street vendors passing through the neighborhood are useful for "top-up" supplies – small

---

[37] *¡Naranja! ¡Naranja dulce, naranja! ¡Naranja dulce!*
[38] *Hay aguacate hay cebolla hay pimiento, ¡la bue-na ca-la-ba-za!*
[39] *¡Llegó el pastelero de 40 centavos! Vecinos, ¡me voy! ¡Me voy! ¡El pastelero de 40 centavos!*

quantities of goods that do not merit a special excursion to the market, or that add to that night's dinner. None of my informants did all their produce shopping from passing vendors, but all of them used them as a kind of mobile and limited "convenience store," buying bits and pieces on a whim or because they forgot on a previous shopping trip.

When larger weekly supplies of fruit, vegetables and other foodstuffs are needed, household managers go to the market to stock up on produce at slightly lower prices. In inner Santiago there are two markets within close proximity of the Tivolí: the *Plaza*, which is 12 blocks north from the center of the neighborhood, and *Trocha y Cristina*, 12 blocks to the southeast.[40] Both of these markets are made up of individual vendors who buy and sell their produce privately. Like the ambulatory vendors, their livelihood was legalized in the early 1990s, and so these two longstanding marketplaces that first featured private vendors, and then become state controlled, are once again the domain of small business. Although not every stallholder might have completed all the paperwork and requirements necessary, selling fruit, vegetables and most kinds of meat is generally considered legal within the formal market space and is carried out publicly. Market stalls are clearly defined by wooden structures and, in the case of *Trocha y Cristina*, include perimeter fencing and concrete shelters in key areas. Prices are fairly fixed, and bargaining is not generally undertaken. The goods sold in the market are from the area surrounding the city of

---

[40] Since the completion of this manuscript, the *Trocha y Cristina* market has closed, and people in the Tivolí use the two other markets described in this chapter.

Santiago, and everything sold is grown or raised on small plots of farmland rather than on large state-run plantations.

There are other markets in more distant areas of the city, but the only Tivolí resident I encountered who regularly used one of these was the indefatigable Fernanda. Weekly, Fernanda travels to a particular state market that sells produce cultivated on military land and picked by young people completing their national service. The goods sold at this market are noticeably cheaper than at any private market, but to reach the market takes about an hour's travel by horse-drawn coach. Returning from the market, Fernanda has to walk with her shopping from the edge of Santiago Bay up the steep hills to the Tivolí. However, Fernanda maintains that the prices make the journey worthwhile and never seems bothered by the extra effort. She was, however, alone among my informants in this judgment.

Dollar Shops: La Shopping

On the central shopping street of Enramadas, a 10-minute walk from the Tivolí, shops selling goods in local pesos (*moneda nacional*) are encrusted with dust. In the dark interiors, one tired woman might sit behind an empty counter, and window displays present one or two objects faded from years in the sunlight. Nobody is shopping; indeed, there is nothing to buy. The shops cower within pre-revolutionary shells and suggest the degree to which American-style shopping was a feature of middle-class life in Santiago of the 1950s. Wooden interiors house islands of glass cabinets; shop staff are marooned with these empty displays with little to do but wait. Samples of the little stock that exists is a combination of locally produced – sachets of talcum powder, mysterious metallic components – and imported goods seemingly leftover from the Soviet period, such as a child-sized pair of *lederhosen*-like overalls that grace the window of one second-hand clothing shop. Although the larger stores have high ceilings and open spaces to combat the stifling heat, few of the ceiling fans crank into life, and temperatures soar in the hotter parts of the day.

In contrast to the lethargy of the peso stores is the dollar (or convertible Cuban peso) grocery shop called the *Bombonera,* a block away from Enramadas Street. In front of the shop there is always a bustle of people looking into the windows, waiting for companions to emerge with a purchase or begging tourists for small change. The *Bombonera* is constantly full, and sometimes there is a queue to get inside. Doormen prevent crowds from entering all at once, check outgoing bags and prevent people from entering if they seem likely to harass foreign customers. Many goods are refrigerated, and the air conditioning offers a welcome respite from the heat and humidity of the streets. Once past the façade, there are no hints of the nineteenth-century structure that houses the shop; blank modern panels cover the walls and ceilings, white tiles surface the floor and fluorescent lights fill the space. Salespeople are dressed in navy outfits provided by the management and are busy conversing with the constant flow of acquaintances or each other as shoppers struggle to get their attention.

The most obvious feature of the *Bombonera* apart from the crowds is the quantity of stock that fills the shelves. Although it has fewer groceries than an average corner shop in London or New York, the *Bombonera* boasts the greatest range of food products available in central Santiago. Much of the business is geared to tourist needs: bottled water, expensive rum, soft drinks and beer. Other groceries serve a mix of tourists and better-off Cubans who can afford such items as pasta or tomato paste. Occasional odd items appear, such as vegan cheese for US $4, mussels for US$ 8 per can, or supersized jars of capers for US $12. For the residents of the Tivoli, although the *Bombonera* and similar dollar shops are the major source of non-food groceries such as toothpaste and shampoo, food shopping in dollar stores is restricted to small investments that supplement or enrich the "basic" food shopping:

> *Nilda:* [I go] maybe once a month, once every 20 days, depending, because sometimes I go to the dollar shop but to buy 4 sachets of stock to make soup, you know? Or maybe 15 days later I go, and buy some spices. But it's not…if I go twice [in a month] it's to buy something minimal, isn't it, it's not really proper food.

Dollar shops offer goods one simply cannot acquire in any other way. Historically they stocked imported and specialty goods for foreign diplomats and authorized visitors to socialist Cuba. With the Special Period local residents could openly use dollars, and dollar stores became the source of important commodities that were longer supplied through the ration system. At present many stocked goods are made in Cuba, but require processing or packaging that separates them from the categories of food allocated in pesos. Odalys, for example, buys cubes of chicken stock from dollar shops, while Fernanda buys packets of soft drink powder to make at home, some of which she sells to neighbors. Odalys also buys tomato purée from dollar shops if she cannot get a good quality alternative from one of her contacts in the neighborhood, and regularly buys spaghetti as well. In a typical shopping week for the women of the Tivolí, no more than US$1 would be spent on average on food in dollar shops, and many of these items would be the first cut in times of economic hardship as they are the extras that make a diet more interesting but not basic necessities.

City Farming: Domestic Production and Home-Grown Food

Despite the emphasis of Cuban socialism on industrial development, urban infrastructure and modernity, residents of city communities such as the Tivolí recognize the greater food security enjoyed by citizens in rural Cuba.[41] With the

---

[41] There is evidence that even in prosperous periods of the revolution, rural Cubans would frequently give or sell excess fruit, vegetables and meat from land allocated for domestic production to relatives and other residents of cities who otherwise depended upon the vagaries of the state distribution system for fresh produce (Benjamin, Collins & Scott 1986: 43-4). The breakdown of services and infrastructure in the post-

Special Period, residents in urban areas adopted many of the domestic production skills associated with rural life in order to offset acute food shortages. Because rural and traditional skills have become so useful in food for the household in urban areas, the two women (of the six households featured in this chapter) who expressed the least anxiety about shopping for food had grown up in the countryside, and had close relatives living on small farms.

> *Fernanda*: Up on the roof I have some chickens, and I am keeping two pigs. We had another one that we slaughtered in May, and that way we didn't have to worry about meat. We cut it up and froze it, and gave some to people around here. They let us know if they want some before we slaughter the pig. And we use the lard for cooking. So that way food isn't really a problem for us.
>
> *Elisabeth*: We raise pigs. Here in the patio we have a big pig.
>
> *Anna*: Do you grow vegetables too?

Soviet period further emphasized the advantages of rural Cubans in food security; acute food shortages experienced in cities in the 1990s led many urban workers to seek work in rural areas. In a study of re-peasantization in Cuba after 1990, Laura Enríquez found that 25% of her sample of farmers had been urban workers before 1990 and that they reported guaranteed access to food as the major incentive to become farmers (2003). Although her study concluded that farmers near Santiago were worse off economically than their counterparts in Havana province, all farmers were receiving better economic and material benefits than the average urban salary earner.

Elisabeth: No, not here. We don't have a big
enough patio. But my parents do; they raise pigs,
grow *fongo* plantains, bananas, pumpkin,
malanga, um…spices. I do have a little bed of
coriander [*cilantro*]. I really love it. And the
things that they [parents] grow, they send to us,
or we go there and bring it home. And fruits too.
Let's say, every fortnight, sometimes only once
in a month – when you can go. It's not a fixed
thing.

Elisabeth and Fernanda both moved to the city for their
husbands' work, and their rural upbringing seemed to
prepare them especially well for post-Soviet urban living.
Not only did they have the skills to raise their own
livestock, thereby securing a steady supply of cheap meat,
but they also benefited from regular supplies of farm
produce brought by country relatives. Contemporary life
seems to have created an interesting inversion in the
privileging of urban knowledge over rural knowledge;
whereas in the earliest years of the revolution, many of the
rural poor relocated to the city were ill-prepared to cope
with the demands of a "highly organized and secular
society" (Lewis, Lewis & Rigdon 1978:532), today having
rural contacts and farm know-how is a powerful advantage
in managing urban domestic economies.[42]

---

[42] These relative difficulties of urban life and the renewed advantages
of rural life in Cuba can be seen to have parallels with other urban
communities in Latin America. For example, González de la Rocha
notes that the rural poor often benefit from access to land and home
production that offsets poverty in ways that the urban poor cannot.

Although rural knowledge is tremendously useful for successful city living in contemporary Cuba, it is important to note that the women of the Tivolí are not engaged in the typical rural or peasant economy that many anthropologists have studied in the Latin American region. Studies of household economies identified by anthropologists in rural Colombia, or the Ecuadorian Andes, to take just two excellent examples, reveal a relationship to food and consumption that is utterly different from the experience of Cuban city dwellers (Gudeman & Rivera 1990; Weismantel 1988). Rural Colombians and Ecuadorians acknowledge the close relationship between land, their physical labor and food consumption, but for residents of the Tivolí, food is primarily something that comes from shops and delivery trucks, rather than something that one grows or processes oneself.[43] Even those in rural Cuba are unlikely to recognize the realities that Gudeman & Rivera report in rural Colombia. In Cuba, the agricultural economy historically dominated by sugar was transformed under socialist planning, and the municipality of Santiago de Cuba allowed for few privately managed small farms (Enríquez 1994:12-14; Enríquez 2003).

Most of Latin America has higher rates of absolute poverty in urban than rural areas; that is, more poor people live in cities than in the country, although relative poverty remains higher in rural communities (1995:16).

[43] At the same time, I do not assume the existence of "intact" localized rural domestic economies elsewhere in Latin America. For example, Weismantel's study of food and gender among the Zumbuaga of the Andes discusses a range of mass-produced purchased foods such as noodles, oatmeal and wheat flour that are "fully integrated into indigenous foodways" (Weismantel 1988:96).

Illegal but Respectable: The Moral Complexities of Black and Grey Markets

Purchasing goods from vendors meshes legal and illegal transactions, creating a commercial environment with varying degrees of trust. In the Tivolí, vendors offer goods literally from the front doorstep or, in the case of illicit goods, just within the front door. Particularly in the market at *Trocha y Cristina*, the side-by-side nature of the black and legal markets is starkly apparent. The legalization of private selling has enabled and obfuscated an active black market, which is a core source of consumption activity in Santiago de Cuba.

Since 1993, fruits and vegetables, chickens and pigs as well as more elaborate products made from purchased ingredients, such as the biscuits and cakes sometimes sold on footpaths or in front of houses, can be produced and sold legally. However, the state still monopolizes the production and cultivation of large-scale agricultural and commercial products so that many common transactions between individuals parties for items such as processed meats, cheeses or ice cream rely on pilfered goods and remain illegal transactions (Pérez-Lopez 1995:63-9,85). The two products most forbidden on the private market are beef and seafood. All cows are officially the property of the Cuban state and, although individual farmers may raise cows on behalf of the state and use the dairy products to which they would not otherwise have access, no cow can be sold or eaten privately, and every cow's death must be officially accounted for. Punishments for possessing and selling beef are severe (Pérez-Lopez 1995:69). Nevertheless, people can buy beef on the black market under a veil of secrecy. Regular vendors of chicken or other products may arrive at the doorstep with a container that, when the seller has safely entered the house, is revealed to contain beef fillets. In urban areas such as Santiago these vendors are more likely to have access to the larders of government restaurants where beef is served legally than to farmers raising cattle in the countryside.

Fish and shellfish are considered slightly less dangerous to buy and sell than beef, but transactions with them are still generally covert operations. Although Santiago de Cuba is a seaside city, seafood makes up remarkably little of the local diet. Local fishermen work for the state and private fishing, while not punishable to the extremes of beef trading, is not legal. However, many fishermen do retain private hauls that they sell on the black market to individuals and to the owners of *paladar* private restaurants. In the *Trocha y Cristina* market, on the edges of the marketplace among the legal and semi-legal vendors, waiting seafood dealers compete for business. Usually a person looking to buy fish would be taken to one of the houses along the nearby wharf where the fish or shellfish is stored, and the deal is made away from the public gaze. Such transactions are seen as risky for the consumer as these seafood dealers are considered to be hustlers capable of overcharging or selling damaged or unhealthy goods. Buyers throughout Santiago prefer to go to *Trocha y Cristina* for fish only when they know a specific family or fisherman with whom they have built a relationship of trust. In any case, under-the-counter seafood is not a frequent dietary feature in the Tívolí because it tends to be more expensive than chicken or pork, unless it is fish sold through the state rationing outlets, as mentioned by Reina above. Shellfish in particular is extremely expensive and out of reach for most Cubans; prawns and particularly lobsters are almost as dangerous to sell as beef because the government reserves 100% of local shellfish for the tourist industry. As a result, the only people I met in the Tívolí with the means to regularly buy shellfish were the owners of a restaurant who offered lobster to tourists at US $12 per person.

The vendors who sell meat and seafood door to door are referred to customers through a network of acquaintances. Dominga's adoptive daughter Odalys, who receives enough economic support from her daughters to feed her extended family with relatively few sacrifices, buys the majority of her protein in this way, most commonly chicken or pork. As her house is known to be a good sales opportunity, several vendors visit her whenever they have meat to sell. Although she cannot be certain who or what will arrive on any given day, she has enough contacts to rely on this system as her main source of meat, which is served most days in her household. Similarly, Nilda has two main vendors who visit her at unscheduled times to sell her meat and fish. Nilda relies less on this method than Odalys as she is rarely at home during the day and misses many opportunities to buy outside shops and marketplaces. Nilda has only recently received income that allows her to buy extra meat so she has not yet built the extensive network of contacts. Nilda buys chicken from a young man who was sent to her by a neighbor; she doesn't know his name or where he lives but, as he was sent by someone she trusts, she bought chicken from him two or three times and he started coming more regularly to her house. The other covert vendor from whom Nilda bought was a fisherman from a coastal town to the west of Santiago, whose aunt was another neighbor. When he leaves Santiago for home, he takes an order from Nilda for fish, and she expects his delivery on an approximate date (such as "on the weekend" or "in about 10 days"). Sometimes conditions such as the weather, transport problems or a change in plans disrupt the arrangement. However, when the fisherman does return to visit his aunt, he walks up the block to Nilda's and comes inside to give her the fish, which she promptly pays for at a price negotiated on the spot but basically agreed beforehand. Nilda explained that she is much more comfortable with this vendor than with the meat vendor because she has known his family for many years and trusts the source of the fish.

Women in the Tivolí must cultivate relationships of trust to enable their shopping needs to be met despite ongoing shortages and the risk of punishment. As Sampson recognized in the case of Eastern European consumers, the key to procuring anything in the informal or "second" economies that tend to emerge under socialism is to establish some kind of private relationship with the seller (Sampson 1987:130). With the absence of an efficient legal framework to ensure that the right goods are sold at the right price, people rely on knowing each other personally, or knowing people in common, to minimize the risk involved in informal sales and exchanges. Because an informal transaction relies on the integrity of the participants, women in the Tivolí prefer to build a personal relationship with the people from whom they buy. The state cannot be trusted to provide goods, and so people prefer to put their trust in other people to keep food and groceries coming into the house. Rather than treating encounters with sellers as merely business, they cultivate relationships with "their" vendors. This also extends to the state shops, where maintaining a relationship with a salesperson may allow goods to be put aside or insider information about when goods will be in stock (Berdahl 1999:120, Burikova 2003).

Damian Fernández has argued that trusting other people in order to get things done in Cuba necessarily involves the risk of deception: "In Cuba transactions in the informal [economy] carry a level of stress, fear and vulnerability vis-à-vis the unknown other, because participants are well aware of the extensive security apparatus and the risks involved in conducting illegal transactions. Who is to say that your new *socio* or *socia* is not an undercover security agent?" (Fernández 2000:111). My conversations with consumers suggest that most fears related to the quality of goods rather than the possibility of state prosecution.

> *Yanet:* With meat, you have to know who you're dealing with. Cornflour, you really have to know them; there was a case around here where the sellers put something in it and you know, a little boy died. There have been a lot of cases of tomato puree made with ground-up bricks and who knows what mixed in it; they don't think about the damage they could be doing to the people who consume it. So that's why I'm more

> fussy with these things. The things to be fussiest
> about in buying food is knowing the people.

Yanet is explaining a common perspective: In the context
of scarcity Cuban consumers feel obliged to take risks in
making everyday purchases. Even for consumers not
especially worried about police persecution for black-
market trading, concerns about the safety and origin of
soap, tomato paste and seafood demonstrate that the
informal economy is a space of mistrust and insecurity that
depends on relations of trust to provide security against
state shortages.

As the women in this chapter indicated, acquiring goods
through informal means is standard daily practice. As many
of these informal exchanges are legal, or technically illegal
but generally tolerated, people are quite open about the
large amount of their domestic provisioning that is met by
informal means. Marisa Wilson has noted with reference to
provisioning in Cuba that "legal rules may be broken in
everyday life, but there is moral difference in the local
economy between acceptable and unacceptable illegal
activity, a distinction which stems from the wider cultural
system" (2009b:175). Elisabeth had no hesitation in
discussing her daily purchases from street vendors,
Fernanda happily explained the economic benefits of
rearing pigs on her roof and Reina frankly admitted the
importance of her sister's passing on of rationed soap.
Other transactions that are undoubtedly illegal but
widespread are referred to with more discretion but are
understood to be a necessary part of life. When Yanet and
her mother talked about buying black-market cooking oil,

or when Nilda shared her sources of black-market seafood, these topics were not treated as terrible secrets. Black market transactions were conducted by upstanding members of the Tivolí community. Both Nilda and Yanet's mother are citizens who generally (if not always enthusiastically) fulfill their duties to the socialist state; they are salaried professionals, community meeting attendees, union members and the devoted mothers of polite, well-educated youths. Thus, although there are illegal and secret businesses in the informal sector referred to that are rarely acknowledged in the presence of a foreign anthropologist, transactions that are morally reprehensible and deeply illegal are not the stuff of everyday household consumption.[44]

The Benefits of Ambiguity in a Socialist Economy

Alena Ledeneva described the gifting-trading processes of *blat* in Soviet Russia, transactions that can be represented as a gift or exchange, as characteristic of socialist societies (1998). Emphasizing the social relationship between buyer and seller enables what would otherwise be commerce to take place without acknowledging that black- (or grey-) market activity has occurred. In contemporary Cuba it is

---

[44] One example of illegal consumption that would be clearly unacceptable to many of the women in the Tivolí is marijuana consumption (although their children might feel differently). In contrast, the consumption of black market food would be only frowned upon by the most hard-line of Communists, and even they are likely to quietly partake of black market foods with regularity.

hard to know what exactly is legal and illegal and, as shown, many of the transactions by women in the Tivolí could arguably fall on either side of the legal divide. When Elisabeth buys okra from a vendor, who is to say whether the vendor has paid her monthly fee? And when Reina explains that her husband has cooking oil from his bakery, who knows if the oil was stolen? When Odalys serves chicken for dinner, who knows if her rations were used up and she bought extra chicken on the black market? The constant blurring of boundaries between formal and informal, legal and illegal, moral and immoral is a characteristic feature of everyday life in Cuba, as evidenced by the roundabout ways in which women habitually discuss their consumption practices. As Ledeneva argued in the case of *blat*, concepts operating in daily life in Soviet Russia had potential for confusion, thus allowing relationships, words and practices to evade the black-and-white restrictions of socialist ideology, just as in daily life in contemporary Cuba. Urban residents living in tenuous circumstances cannot rely on support from kin dispersed across space, have minimal access to primary sources of production and are always vulnerable to the anonymity and unpredictability of city living (see also Hart 2000).[45] In the Tivolí, daily life depends upon the cultivation of relationships that are neither entirely friendship nor entirely business, in which the language of kinship and personal obligation can be used to offset or disguise the mercenary aspects of the relationship and, conversely, in which the

---

[45] Keith Hart's (2000) research on trust among the Frafras in Accra similarly suggests that trust is what characterizes relationships that fall between the ideals of kinship and contract.

cold logic of business can be used to minimize personal obligations to one another. The need to constantly assess the trustworthiness of others is not confined to consumption but can also be seen in other areas, such as caring for other people's children, borrowing and lending money and in other activities often referred to in social research as "mutual aid." It is significant that almost all examples of mutual aid are between neighbors, acquaintances and friends who are emotionally close. Although family are frequently relied upon for support, mutual assistance between friends and neighbors is more likely to involve donating time or labor than borrowing, lending or giving material goods. At the same time that women in the Tivolí try to maintain good relationships with people who are able to help them obtain goods, many also warn of the need to be vigilant against thieves or people who will take advantage of them (*abusar*). Relying on friends and acquaintances is also a hedge to leaving oneself vulnerable to sharing goods and support with untrustworthy acquaintances.

In Cuba, as throughout collapsing socialist Europe in the 1980s and 1990s, people depend upon the informal economy because of the basic failures of the formal economy. However, because the informal economy depends on the structures and resources of the formal economy, an expanding informal economy diverts even more goods from the formal economy and exacerbates the economy of shortages. At the same time, by tolerating the existence of an informal economy and by legalizing certain kinds of private commerce, the Cuban state has been able to maintain the ideology and rhetoric of socialism. Contemporary Cuban economy is an example of how the contradictions central to life under "actually existing socialism" may enable maintenance of a socialist state (Verdery 1996:27, Sampson 1987:122, Ledeneva 1998:3 Pérez-Lopez 1995:1).

Although socialism may influence the forms that informal markets take, there are many other market systems in which a weakness of the state enables informal economies to prosper. Research in West Africa and Latin America, for example, has described communities in which many economic practices have minimal interaction with state bureaucracies (Hart 1973; Castells & Portes 1989). Other ethnographies have demonstrated that affluent capitalist economies have important informal economic sectors that may compensate for formal sector opportunities in marginalized areas (as Mollona found in Sheffield, 2005), exploit social capital to support new migrant communities (as Stoller notes in his research on African traders in New York City, 1996) or circumvent bureaucracy in such a way that it effectively bolsters the formal economy (as Castells & Portes describe with reference to Italy, 1989). What seems to distinguish an informal market from a traditional or peasant market in these examples, and also in the substantial research on informal markets in Latin America, is a parallel formal market, whether capitalist or socialist. Tivolí women are therefore not alone in combining official institutions and informal networks for everyday consumption although Santiago has local forms of informal trade that that can be substantially different from informal economies elsewhere. Nor are Cubans alone in using social networks as a useful strategy for consumption both formal and informal. Consumers in all societies, whether socialist, capitalist or otherwise cultivate personal relationships that defuse the social distance that trade is seen to create. Nevertheless, the emphasis in socialist states on the state-managed distribution of goods does seem to have a particular counter effect in that many socialist consumers particularly value their personal networks as a resource to offset state-imposed constraints. Several anthropologists studying the transition to post-socialism in Central and Eastern Europe recognized that in much of the socialist era and communities, "social connections were the principal means of obtaining scarce consumer goods and services" (Berdahl 1999:115). The literature demonstrates that in socialist Russia, East Germany, Romania and Hungary, gifts, barter and bribes were at least as common as commercial shopping for everyday groceries (Ledeneva 1998; Berdahl 1999:118-20; Verdery 1996:27-9; Kenedi 1981). As one of Daphne Berdahl's informants in a newly reunified Germany explained, in a socialist economy "Money actually did help you: it helped maintain the connections! But the connections were most important" (1999:120, see also Sampson 1987:131).

To successfully negotiate the informal economy, women in the Tivolí employ considerable knowledge. They must know prices before negotiating them, as Nilda demonstrated in purchasing black market seafood. They must know the sources of goods without asking, as Yanet's mother explained in reference to oil. They must use wisdom in selecting trustworthy sources and products, and in some instances know to pay a higher price in order to save time, as Elisabeth did in purchasing from street vendors. In other cases, investing time is a sensible trade-off for saving some money, as Fernanda decided in traveling to the military market. The most banal of consumption practices require not only a significant investment of time and exertion, but also a complex body of knowledge that is constantly being revised in the changing political and economic circumstances of Cuba. Consumers are aware that their routines and strategies are vulnerable to the vagaries of state distribution policies, weak infrastructure and environmental hazards. Consequently, even the most essential practices of daily consumption – such as the buying, preparation and eating of food – can be the source of distress, anxiety or outrage, precisely because it is also the source of strength, nourishment, and comfort.

Food Anxiety and Food Sharing: The Fear of Hunger and Food Hiding

Although five of the six families whose household spending I studied reported regular difficulties in shopping for food, only one household reported skipped meals or hunger on a semi-regular basis. Furthermore, all families reported that, although they experienced chronic hunger in the mid 1990s, often with weight loss and health problems associated with poor nutrition, by 2004 their average food intake was substantially better. Nonetheless, memories of hunger were fresh in the minds of many. When I started conversations about current food consumption, stories of the hunger experienced the 1990s were invariably raised for comparison.

Although some of the poorest residents of the Tivolí in 2004 served smaller meals or skipped meals at the end of a ration period, for the most part hunger and undernourishment of the sort defined by such institutions as the World Food Program were not widespread. Yet talk of hunger remained prevalent. In research on the introduction of food aid to Nicaragua in the 1980s, which has some interesting parallels to the Cuba, Stephanie Linkogle notes that "hunger is not merely the absence of food. It is the failure of a set of relationships which condition not only the quality, quantity and type of foods available but also the consumption choices that are made within this framework" (Linkogle 1998:94).[46] Linkogle's work in Nicaragua provides a useful clue to understanding how the idea of ongoing scarcity coexists with preferences, distastes and selectiveness in food consumption in Cuba. This important distinction between hunger as evidence of malnutrition and hunger as a dissatisfaction with food choices is central to how Cubans experience food scarcity. Even in the 1980s, a period remembered by my informants as offering a vast variety of foods, nutritionists Benjamin, Collins and Scott emphasized that, although hunger and malnutrition had

---

[46] Linkogle's work notes that the introduction of soy proteins as a form of international food aid in Sandinista Nicaragua met with a very similar reaction to that in Cuba. As in Cuba, meat is the prized protein and soy is not considered genuine "strong" food (1998).

been eradicated, citizens complained about going hungry or lacking food options not as a matter of nutrition, but of taste and satisfaction. Although nutritional food was available and affordable for everybody, food did not necessarily conform to Cuban conceptions of "real food" or "good food" (Benjamin, Collins & Scott 1986: 91-2).

The perception that food is scarce, or that its supply is insecure, is expressed in the ways that food is stored in households, and in the way that food is exchanged between trusted associates. Anthropologists have noted that sharing food often reflects sharing social networks (see for example Mintz 1986: 3-6; Marshall 1961:231-249). But in contemporary Cuba, although the importance of social networks in purchasing food has been documented, food for household consumption is rarely shared with anyone but close family members or best friends, and sometimes not even with them.[47] Food is not typically offered to casual visitors or even to visiting relatives and close friends; for these occasions coffee would be a standard offering, and sometimes a soft drink or juice, but only rarely would a sweet snack or fruit be served. In general, food is served only at parties that have been planned; offerings typically

---

[47] During the course of my fieldwork, I was offered (or sometimes just served) coffee or juice almost every time I visited households included in this chapter. However, over the months that I visited the Tivolí, I was never invited to a meal in Dora's, Tomasito's, Elisabeth's or Reina's house. I was invited to stay for lunch twice at Fernanda's house (both times I declined) and was once invited to a special lunch at Yanet's house. I once was similarly treated to a (rather lavish) breakfast at Dominga's house. In contrast, at Nilda's house, where I was treated as a member of the extended family, I ate many regular meals and attended several party meals. Other "adoptive family" members who are not included as informants in this study also fed me many times.

consist of cake, pasta salad, biscuits and croquettes. Although such party food is usually presented on a table in view of the guests, the food is apportioned to individual plates by the women of the household and their friends or relatives; several times when I was privy to party planning discussions I was told by women that they did this to ensure that everybody had a fair amount of food and "nobody took too much."

I was struck by a similar instance of controlling portions when one day a cousin from another town unexpectedly visited Dominga and Odalys. I was in the kitchen with Odalys when she pulled out a bottle of export-quality rum from a cupboard and poured a small glass to take to her guest in the living room. Taking the glass back to the kitchen to serve him a second shot, I asked Odalys why she didn't just take the bottle into the living room. She replied in a half-whisper that if she were to put the bottle in front of her cousin, he would not leave the house until he'd drunk it all. Odalys was calculating a balance between hospitality and limiting a valued resource. Although her cousin counted as kin close enough to be offered a special drink, and Odalys wanted to make this special gesture, he was not of the household to such a degree that allowed him total access to her resources.[48]

---

[48] Although for the purposes of this example it is appropriate to include an alcoholic drink such as rum in a section on food, the vast anthropological literature on the role of alcohol would support the observation I made earlier in this chapter that rum is not treated as "food" by Cubans, and its purchase is not generally included by women in domestic economic planning.

Although people in Cuba feel free to visit one another unannounced, and receiving guests hospitably is important and frequent among residents of the Tivolí, food is more likely to be concealed in a Cuban kitchen than shared. Guests who arrive in the middle of a meal may very well be asked to wait on the doorstep or in the front room while the family finishes eating. Or, for example, families who have prepared a meal will wait for guests to leave before they bring out the plates and cutlery and eat. Some of this propensity to withhold, control and hide food can be explained by the prevalent notion of food as a scarce resource. Indeed, stockpiling food and planning months ahead for special food purchases – regular occurrences in the kitchens of the Tivolí– are similar to the food buying practices Berdahl reports as common in socialist East Germany (Berdahl 1999:121).[49] Concerns about when and where food supplies will next arrive are factors in women's decisions about how much food they can share. Family meals are generally made only in sufficient quantities to feed the number of people expected; if unexpected guests arrive, cooks feel, often correctly, that there will not be enough food to go around. Furthermore, the difficulty of acquiring basic staples (such as rice or beans) beyond allocated rations creates challenges and anxieties for hosts who might otherwise be willing to give away quantities of their own food. Although neighbors on good terms will regularly give each other sugar or salt from leftover rations,

---

[49] However, the scale of hoarding that Berdahl reports was achieved only by one of the women included in this chapter (Fernanda), as most women simply could not afford to buy sufficient quantities of food at one time to enable hoarding. Fernanda's well-stocked larder was due more to her rural contacts and skills than to economic capital.

I never observed lending or giving more scarce foodstuffs such as meat, eggs and milk except in close family circles. Such items were, however, sometimes resold to friends and acquaintances.

It is difficult to know how much of this relative restriction of sharing is an outcome of socialist food distribution policies. Kathryn Verdery notes that a lack of food and drink led to a decrease in socializing in Romania (1996:52.55). It is also possible that the reluctance of Cuban women to share their food is a form of resistance to the policies of socialist food distribution that traditionally stigmatize hoarding and ban private trade. Although an unintended outcome of the state distribution of food in Cuba has been an informal economy of barter and trade, another consequence of the state attempts to manage food security has been to increase consumer fears that nationwide shortages must be averted by hoarding whenever possible. However, comparative research has demonstrated that food sharing with visitors and extended kin is common in other societies where food is as scarce, or more so (cf. Mintz & DuBois 2002). While working in the Tivolí, I frequently wondered whether anxiety about food shortages was the only reason why Cubans generally withhold food from all but their closest kin, or whether more longstanding cultural orientations to food were also playing a role. It was only in reading about a community that seemingly bears little relation to urban Cuba – the Gurage of Ethopia – that I started understanding how withholding food from others may in itself be an expression of concern for others. In researching the Gurage, anthropologist William Shack noted that although the

Gurage have intermittent experiences of food shortages, food anxiety is high even when food is readily available. The Gurage eat very little food in public, and never finish the food served to them when visiting others, but frequently hoard food and eat it privately at night (Shack 1997[1971]:128). Reading about the Gurage, I couldn't help but remember the exclamation of relief that Sonia gave one evening after the departure of guests: "At last, we can eat dinner!" I also thought of the many times that I adopted the Cuban habit of lying and claiming that I wasn't hungry to ease the mind of a hostess who probably didn't want to feed me anyway. Such examples might suggest that Cubans are unfriendly or reluctant to build meaningful relationships beyond their immediate family, best friends and romantic partners. However, ethnographic studies of cultural approaches to sharing food and material resources in the Caribbean region, particularly in Jamaica, show otherwise. Sobo argues that in rural Jamaica, "Because kin share wealth, no-one gets rich. Because kin feed each other, no-one becomes thin. Cultural logic has it that people firmly tied into a network of kin are always plump and never wealthy" (Sobo 1997:256). People in Cuba acknowledge a duty to feed their kin and, as Horst and Miller noted in Jamaica, Cubans would generally agree that building relationships with as many people as possible is positive (Horst & Miller 2005: 755-778). Perhaps then, the women of the Tivolí sometimes hide food precisely because they are aware of the need to feed kin; they know that they could not publicly eat without sharing, and so if they feel that if their circumstances do not permit sharing, they would rather go hungry than openly flout their obligation to share food. Perhaps withholding food is partially a testament to the Cuban understanding of food as social; offering food to close kin, and avoiding the refusal of food to a guest. If a visitor were bold enough to actually ask for food (which he or she never would unless they were part of the household's inner circle), it would be unthinkable for a host to refuse to share what food they had. Although sharing a meal is evidence of successful family and love connections, not being offered food may be less a sign of exclusion than a suggestion that you might indeed be in that inner circle except that no food happens to be available just at the moment.

The particular ways in which food is shared, hoarded or hidden are likely shaped by attitudes toward sharing domestic resources that predate the scarcity of the Special Period and seem to be found elsewhere in the Caribbean region (Rosendahl 1997:28-50; Sobo 1997:256-71). In Jamaica the notion of scarcity coupled with a desire for social relationships impels individuals to ask, beg, borrow and visit other people while at the same time minimizing their obligations to offer, donate, lend or invite them in turn. As Odalys demonstrated by rationing her rum, women in the Tivolí recognize that sharing resources and connections with community and extended family can be more of a burden and obligation than a pleasure. However, at the same time that Cuban women withhold or control food and drink in the household, they emphasize that gracious and appropriate behavior should typically include generosity and a willingness to help and share.

Everyday Battles and Heroic Shopping

The stories women tell about grocery shopping in Santiago demonstrate awareness of the impact that state policy has upon their consumption practices, for better and for worse. For consumers in the Tivolí and elsewhere in Cuba, to eat poorly is commonly understood as a failure of socialist distribution, and to eat well is generally seen as a triumph over the obstacles in acquiring diverse and tasty food. The Cuban state has consistently promoted the central role of food and nutrition in the revolutionary agenda; changing and improving the food eaten by the average Cuban was central to the formation of a revolutionary identity (Enríquez 1994:1-4; Benjamin, Collins & Scott 2003:344-53; Linkogle 1998:97-8). Although in earlier years, an adverse food situation effectively mobilized solidarity and support for Cuban socialism, since the 1990s consumers have increasingly blamed national rather than international or ideological factors for the shortages of food and other groceries. Although the ideal of the state as the provider of goods has remained – exemplified by the way people talk of rationed food "arriving" rather than being purchased (*me llegó la carne*, "my meat arrived") – the inability of the government to match socialist discourse with the "arrival" of material goods has been a major, if not the major, source of disillusionment now in Cuba. Having linked revolution and the provision of goods, the credibility of Cuban socialism is now suffering from the association between revolution and the scarcity of goods. As the shopping practices of women in the Tivolí demonstrate, the Cuban state is simultaneously the provider of goods and an obstacle to their provision.

It is important to note that several of the women interviewed also spoke with considerable pride about their abilities to overcome difficulties and to be good mothers and housekeepers. Thus, when women talk about the problems they encounter in their everyday struggle for groceries, it is not all sadness or frustration; sometimes their accounts are also triumphant. Nancy Ries, whose work was discussed in Chapter 2, considered tales of what she calls "heroic shopping" to be an important genre of women's conversation in Russia during *perestroika*. Tales such as that of the Russian grandmother who queued with steely determination for nine hours to buy a bag of sugar constitute a repertoire of tales of woe from which Russian women build a positive identity of overcoming adversity (Ries 1997:51-64). In emphasizing their capacity to overcome obstacles to domestic consumption, women in the Tivolí can be seen as reinforcing traditional notions of womanly virtue, but they may also use their roles as successful women and mothers to challenge the status quo (Chant & Craske 2003:11). When women criticize the current Cuban economy, they do so from the unassailable position of a woman fulfilling her role as provider of sustenance and comfort.

Consumer shortages also provide a space for meaningful social interaction in Cuba. For almost as long as the duration of the revolution, Cuban sociality has been built around the practices of socialist consumption, with systems of queuing for goods, sharing information about where items can be bought, voicing hearty complaints that could not usually be openly expressed about any other aspect of Cuban society (Rosendahl 1997:29; Benjamin, Collins & Scott 1986:44-46,75-77). Consumption of everyday groceries is a space for vigorous discussion and relationships as much as it is a space for sociopolitical critique. The consumption process allows women to accumulate and display powerful social knowledge and provides the basis for a prestigious form of feminine identity. In seeing the provision of food as creating strength and wellbeing in the family, women in Cuba face much hard work to keep their households healthy and "strong." The extreme difficulty of acquiring goods has been a real challenge for women, although the same challenge has created opportunities for women to become heroic consumers. However, opportunities for heroism through resourceful consumption are heroic only because of the risk of failure. Although the most severe outcomes of failing to provide food for consumers are obvious, this chapter has suggested some of the more common ways in which anxieties about food shortages affect social life.

Chapter 4

Interior Revolutions: *Renovations, Furnishings and Domestic Appliances*

The Cuban revolution has been a public event, played out on television and in diplomatic encounters across the globe for over five decades. This public staging of revolution and post-revolution in Cuba continues, as Raúl Castro's leadership of transition has attracted much attention and speculation. Rather than examining public expressions of Cuban politics and identity, in this chapter I focus on the everyday practices and items of domestic life, which are an equally important site from which to analyze politics and identity in contemporary Cuba. Specifically, I trace some transformations in domestic life by examining material culture and the everyday objects that shape the routines and environments of domestic life. I suggest that some of the intricacies and subtleties of how citizens have negotiated decades of political and economic change can be revealed this way, which more conventional forms of politico-economic analysis may not capture. The previous chapter on shopping addressed many practices of maintaining a household, but here attention shifts to the contents of the home and the house itself as an important space in which the materialization of social distinction takes place.

Housing shortages have been a central preoccupation of the Cuban government since the inception of the revolution. Some of the earliest reforms in 1959-1960 capped rents according to income as well as redistributed housing. The 1976 Constitution held adequate housing as a fundamental right of all citizens along with healthcare and education (Del Real & Pertierra 2008). However, in comparison to the gains in health and educational services, housing reform has been sporadic, and housing shortages in cities such as Havana and Santiago remain critical. The government redistributed considerable housing in the early years of the revolution, as departing families left (often sizeable) properties behind and policies limited internal migration to the capital. However, a lack of new developments and a growing and an increasingly long-lived population has long pressured available housing in regional capitals such as Santiago, as well as Havana. Although Santiago de Cuba experienced a rise in the construction of new housing in the 1970s and 1980s, which increased housing capacity by almost 20% (Pérez 2006:280-1), today in neighborhoods such as the Tivolí, a large proportion of households continue to comprise three generations. Houses have not been for sale legally since 1960. Citizens who wish to move must either be awarded new housing by the state (usually in recognition of community or military service), or arrange an authorized housing exchange (*permuta*) with another party. The complications and high stakes involved in such negotiations make the possession and retention of housing the subject of great tension within families and neighborhoods.[50]

---

[50] Oscar Lewis's team devoted over 200 pages of their neighborhood

The shortage of new housing in Cuban cities, and the legal, material and economic obstacles to rebuilding and renovating existing houses, means that for many citizens one frustration of daily life is dissatisfaction with their housing conditions. The physical condition of a house and the practical and aesthetic quality of its contents are often the focus of intense emotional and economic investment. In the years preceding the collapse of the socialist bloc, basic household goods, such as sheets, were available at subsidized prices with rations, and superior or alternative styles available at higher, but manageable, prices in Cuban pesos, *moneda nacional* (Rosendahl 1997:31). Since 1993, almost all household goods, including cleaning products, furniture, towels, soft furnishings and kitchenware, are available only in dollar shops or on the black market. For residents who have managed to prosper in recent years through small businesses, cash bonuses or remittances, the family house is the major focus of improvement and investment, as entire houses are built, rebuilt or illegally bought and sold with black-market dollars.[51]

Extensive literature on the material culture of socialist Europe and Russia has emerged since the 1990s, demonstrating how the cultural life of socialist societies was experienced through housing arrangements, domestic

---

study to interviews about one housing exchange that was listed as a major source of dispute between the residents of a Havana apartment block studied in 1968-70. Similarly, Rosendahl notes that during her research in Cuba in the 1980s, "the biggest conflicts arose when housing was at stake, since shortages are severe" (Rosendahl 1997:38).

[51] That a boom in black market housing has occurred is evidenced by a government offensive in 2000 that resulted in the confiscation of over 2,000 houses from residents who had obtained them illegally (Eckstein 2003:237).

appliances and grocery products as much as through monetary systems, ideological debates or diplomatic encounters.[52] There are key differences between the Cuban and European and former USSR experiences of socialism, particularly with regard to housing aesthetics, practices and objects found in homes. The case for Cuba's "exceptionalism" (Kapcia 2008) is strengthened by contemporary life, and these Cuban particularities are materialized in the contents of average Cuban homes. In talking about and working on their homes, Cubans understand themselves as simultaneously connected to and isolated from the various transnational connections through which their society must be understood. With this in mind, before presenting some Cuban homes and the women in charge of them, I want to outline why examining material goods in homes is an especially useful and important task in contemporary Cuba.

There is now an established set of arguments as to the importance of studying domestic material culture in general; the work of Daniel Miller and others at University College London has connected the interest of archaeology

---

[52] For examples, see Boym, S. 1994. "The Archaeology of Banality: The Soviet Home," *Public Culture* 6:263-292; Buchli, V. 1997. "Krushchev, Modernism, and the Fight against 'Petit-bourgeois' Consciousness in the Soviet Home," *Journal of Design History* 10(2):161-176; Crowley, D. & Reid, S. 2002. "Socialist Spaces: Sites of Everyday Life in the Eastern Bloc," in D. Crowley & S. Reid (Eds.), *Socialist Spaces: Sites of Everyday Life in the Eastern Bloc*. Oxford: Berg; Oldenziel, R. & Zachmann, K. 2009. "Kitchens as Technology and Politics: An Introduction," in R. Oldenziel & K. Zachmann (Eds.), *Cold War Kitchen: Americanization, Technology and European Users*. Cambridge and London: MIT Press.

in the cultural lives of objects to contemporary globalized communities in which most objects are mass produced. Miller suggests that in the contemporary world mass consumption is the primary site through which people creatively appropriate objects to make sense of themselves and the world in which they live (1987). In parallel developments, Pierre Bourdieu (1984) has called attention to domestic goods in the articulation of status and the representation of class ideology, and Michel De Certeau's phenomenological approach to the exploration of everyday life emphasizes the potential of daily domestic acts as forms of political engagement (1998). More broadly, housing, vernacular architecture and home interiors are recognized as bringing together architectural historians, anthropologists, industrial designers and sociologists because it is in domestic spaces that religious, cosmological and political ideas are often experienced and materialized in everyday life (St George 2006). Domestic spaces are especially attractive to scholars looking to understand non-elite society, and so the study of vernacular material forms and everyday consumer goods is often allied with the study of marginalized groups, among them women, indigenous peoples and postcolonial societies (cf. Preston Blier 2006). Domestic objects are brought into a house in particular economic, political and social contexts that can imbue the same object with different meanings across cultures, or between different households in the same culture. Furthermore, the consumers of these objects see their home furnishings as representative of their life histories, and even of political and economic histories. This chapter shows how contemporary Cubans talk and think about domestic material goods not only as functional items but also for what they represent.

The refrigerator is prized for its capacity to keep food from spoiling, but it can also be evidence of successful parenting (as when a well-to-do daughter sends money from abroad for a new model), a tool in displaying gracious hospitality (because cold water can be served to guests), a memory of commitment to socialist activism (when obtained through state schemes) or a reminder of the vulnerability of household wellbeing (when it breaks down and repairs are unaffordable). These multiple responses to the presence of a refrigerator are topics for open conversation, reflection and agitation.

The Work of Living Rooms: Domestic Interiors as Moral Biography

As the economic and ideological parameters of Cuban society change, the winners and losers in the contemporary economy are frequently evidenced in the changes and improvements – or increasing destitution—observable in their domestic spaces. The living room contents of residents in the Tivolí reveal a social map of the ways Cubans negotiate the logistics of everyday life, with varying degrees of success. In this way, the biographies of living room objects are interpreted by the women who own them as a means for constructing their own moral biographies (Silverstone & Hirsch, 1992; Kopytoff 1988).

Dominga's living room is a wonderful example of what I would term a "successful" Tivolí living room; that is, a living room that represents the aesthetic ideals of the community, contains all major decorative features frequently found in the homes of the area and reflects the high, but not excessively high, status of its occupants. Although Dominga's home is not large, a considerable portion of the house is an open living and dining area. Entering the front door, the visitor faces the living room, featuring a typical configuration of a long wooden bench instead of a sofa and three wooden armchairs, one of which is a rocking chair (*balance*). Although vinyl sofas can occasionally be found, living room sets are more usually made of wood, using designs that have changed remarkably little from the early twentieth-century furniture found in older homes.

Fig. 11 *An older wooden living room set*

In Dominga's home, as in others, the *balance* is the domain of the matriarch at rest, and it is from her rocking chair that Dominga tends to survey the street and converse with guests. Seating is grouped around a low table, and in one corner on a stand are a television and video recorder. The video recorder is covered with a decorative cloth, and lace doilies decorate the coffee table, which is rarely used despite its central position. Also on top of this coffee table sits a small basket with a bouquet of artificial flowers: pink roses and baby's breath. Indeed, artificial roses (this time yellow) also adorn the dining table, and two small tables in corners of the living room are decorated with vases with artificial sunflowers and carnations. On the wooden bench rest several cushions, covered by Dominga in red floral prints, and a tall electric fan is by the bench, with a small table holding carnations and a black ceramic swan.

A set of shelves marks the division between the living and dining spaces of Dominga's front room; these shelves are tall but quite narrow, and exist specifically to display treasures. Along one shelf a representative selection is assembled. First a homemade calendar sits next to a small potted plant and a photograph of Odalys's baby granddaughter. Next are three plaster dogs with bobbing heads, a figurine of a lady in an ornate ball gown and a pink bird about to take flight. These are followed by an elephant, a white cartoonish cat, a small vase with a single pink rose, a white horse with a dainty leg in the air, a white and pink ceramic swan, two more figurines dressed for court, a ballerina in a gold-trimmed tutu, and a set of three slim ladies in long flowing gowns looking pensive, baskets in hand. Other shelves are just as densely packed. Admittedly, this array of goods is larger than that in most living rooms, but nevertheless Dominga's shelf is an excellent indication of the range and style of much Cuban interior decoration. Building such a collection of small objects, usually with feminine elegance (pensive ladies, gowns, roses and swans) is the result of many years of Dominga's dedication to her home. I was told by a proud Odalys that almost all of the display were gifts and many from abroad, suggesting that Dominga's décor is also a reflection of her friend-filled global network. Other more practical motives also explain the abundance of small decorative items in Cuban living rooms: miniature ornaments are relatively inexpensive and can be bought over a long period of time, and as gifts they weigh little in the suitcases of people who bring them from abroad.

The walls of Dominga's living room, although not as densely decorated as the shelves and tables, add layers of color and texture to the space. On one wall, above the sunflowers, hang two small bright landscapes and a large, heavy-framed portrait of Jesus that is especially dear to Dominga. On another wall, above the sofa, is a tapestry.[53]

---

[53] This tapestry is an example of a genre of wall hangings that are machine made, brightly colored and typically depict fantastic animal scenes, such as green-eyed tigers in front of waterfalls, lions on sweeping plains or antelope on mountaintops. Early examples of these tapestries were brought primarily from the Middle East and the Soviet Union by Cubans returning from international missions. As they were so popular, cheaper versions have periodically become periodically available in dollar stores since the beginning of the Special Period, and can be found in many Cuban homes.

In the dining area, many items are squeezed into a rather small space: an upright piano, a large dining table with six chairs that complement the living room seating and a new refrigerator crowd the little room. The dining table is covered in a white lacy tablecloth and in addition to the meals served at lunchtime, Odalys uses this table to calculate her bills and record various activities. On top of the piano is a wedding photograph in an ornate silver frame of Dominga with her husband, and the piano is covered in doilies, many of them crocheted by Dominga, who is known among older residents for her handiwork. Finally, to the left of the living room is a long curtain of white, slightly transparent floral fabric, which conceals the bedrooms of Odalys' granddaughter and Dominga. At the back of the dining area is the small internal patio, which connects to the more private spaces of the kitchen and bathroom.

In short, within the small area of Dominga's front room almost the entire repertoire of typical Cuban domestic material culture can be found. As if to reflect how the different political and economic phases of Cuba's modern history have transformed the aesthetics of everyday life, Dominga's living room offers traces of the sources and symbols of prestige found in Cuban domestic interiors. Items carefully preserved from before the revolution, such as the piano bought from a neighbor, the hand-tinted wedding photograph and even the beams of the house structure indicate a modest but admirable acquisition of goods in the early years of Dominga's domestic life. Many of the handicrafts and the crocheted items are products of the senior citizens groups with which Dominga is heavily involved. And finally, the domestic technologies that mark Dominga's house as relatively comfortable – the electric fan, the video recorder and the new refrigerator – are symbols of Special Period affluence, largely provided by the Havana earnings of Odalys's daughter. The aspirations and aesthetics of Dominga's living room capture effectively the transformations in the quest for respectability among the women of the Tivolí.

Fig.12 *Living room decor*

Some living rooms in the neighborhood provide a striking contrast to the ornament-filled interior of Dominga's house. The living room of Reina's house is minimally decorated and does not follow the aesthetic of "on display." Reina's house provides an interesting contrast in its design and furnishings to Dominga's house, as well as how she relates to her domestic space. Reina's house is a small set of rooms built into the side of a larger colonial home. Access is through a side passage so that Reina cannot see the street from her home. The house is extremely dark and poorly ventilated, as the only source of air and natural light comes from the front door and window; the back and side walls are against the main house, and two more stories are on top of Reina's home so that one feels almost underground. As usual, one enters the living room from the front door, and the entire house can be seen from here, although Reina creates some privacy in the two bedrooms with curtains. To the left of the front door is a tiny cement bathroom containing a toilet, tap and bucket, and further along to the left is a slightly larger kitchen area, with one small counter and a stovetop. The Soviet-era refrigerator does not fit in the kitchen, so it sits nearby in the living area, which is common in Tivolí homes.

Reina's living room has a set of wooden chairs (including one long wooden bench) and a rocking chair usually occupied by her ailing grandmother. A low table and a buffet counter housing a black and white television are the only other furnishings in the room. The buffet stores some items such as plates and glasses, and these are behind a closed cupboard, not on display. On Reina's walls are only a few items: a calendar, a magazine cutout and a stopped clock. Photographs, soft furnishings and ornaments are absent, and the walls are unpainted.

Although the interior of Reina's house is dilapidated, the floors and surfaces were extremely clean every time I visited (as in every home I visited in the Tivolí); Reina spends much of her time cleaning the house and laundering, particularly because her grandmother's incontinence creates extra work. One day when I visited unannounced, Reina met me at her front door and apologized that she could not invite me into the house because her grandmother was sick and Reina had not yet cleaned everything. Reina worked on her house as much as her neighbors, but as she explained, she does not really think about the aesthetics of her house because household routines and the stress of affording food have higher priority. Reina was generally not interested in talking about her house; although she had ideas about how things might be better, thoughts of improving her home seemed so remote that they were barely worth discussing.

If Dominga's living room contents trace the biography of a successful woman who has adeptly navigated transformations in Cuba and become a respected member of the community, then Reina's living room can represent her failure to meet some criteria of success. Dominga's domestic interior shows her to have succeeded on many fronts: as a wife, as a worker, as a revolutionary and now as the indirect recipient of a dollar income. In contrast, Reina's living room contains no family photos or heirlooms, although the furniture came from her grandmother, and she does maintain close contact with various family members. The absence of most Soviet-era technologies suggests that neither she nor her father undertook the required community work or workplace duties required to acquire household items through the credit voucher system in the 1970s and 1980s. Reina has not fared much better recently as she has no close relatives abroad to send remittances, and her casual government work does not intersect with the dollar-yielding industries of tourism.

Despite the shortage and homogeneity of resources in contemporary Cuba, people build their material environments in distinctive ways to indicate status and differentiate themselves from others. Indeed, because of shortages small differences between households are markedly significant. Dominga and Reina can be seen at two ends of a spectrum between certain privileged forms of gendered activity and social status.[54] Caring about domestic interiors is an important component of idealized feminine identities and of course indicates that one has the material and emotional resources to be able to care about such things. Therefore, the components that make a successful domestic space do not merely reflect the monetary wealth of residents; in fact, many women who invest the most energy in their houses and whose living rooms are most admired are not the wealthiest residents (although they are not the poorest). Dominga in her success and Reina in her lack of it display an orientation to the home through their work on it; although Reina is unable to acquire decorative goods, she constantly cleans her house and emphasizes eventually improving the basic conditions of the space. In

---

[54] It will of course be noted by scholars working elsewhere in the Americas that by Latin American standards, the material difference between Dominga, who is among the most comfortable of residents in the neighborhood, and Reina, among the least, is relatively narrow.

interviews, Reina declared her lack of interest in decorations, but she did have a list of appliances in mind that she hoped to acquire as well as a medium-term plan to renovate her kitchen and bathroom. Neither woman is boastful of her space and both can be seen as dignified (*dignas*) in their approach to housekeeping. This point is crucial in understanding how women view one another through their domestic spaces: Although the material success of a household can be mapped through an inventory of living room contents, for Cuban women, being unable to ornately furnish a house does not necessarily mean that a woman lives without dignity, as long as her household practices demonstrate her commitment to cleanliness and order. The respectability of women is not measured only by the material goods in their houses, but also by attitudes toward the goods and practices within the house.

Dollar Store Gifts, Bourgeois Relics and Socialist Appliances: Categories of Domestic Objects

Residents use many different strategies to acquire the goods that fill their houses, but three types of acquisition relate to the three phases of recent history that have affected domestic furnishings. Recently acquired household items are generally the result of a gift or a cash purchase. Although gifts are frequently brought from outside the community, most cash purchases are made within the city of Santiago de Cuba or in the neighborhood. However, a considerable proportion of the material culture in houses predates this period; most of these objects arrived either through inheritance of goods acquired before the revolution or through "earning" (*ganar*) of domestic commodities in the Soviet period.[55]

Remittances and gifts from overseas constitute a significant part of domestic economies in contemporary Cuba. Indeed, these are recognized as the most important determinant of wealth. Consequently, it is not surprising that many of the objects that adorn the homes of residents are gifts from family members abroad or are bought with money sent from abroad. I have already mentioned that in Dominga's house it is a source of some pride that many of the treasures in her living room were gifts from friends and relatives returning from other countries. In Nilda's house as well, old magazines – read many times over – brought by friends and neighbors from Spain, Mexico and Venezuela are stacked on a shelf in the living room. Similarly, in Fernanda's living room the tapestry that dominates the largest wall was brought as a gift from the United States by Fernanda's brother-in-law. Appliances such as digital recorders and computers are sometimes brought from abroad by returning emigrants or overseas contract workers. However, more frequently domestic items are bought in Cuban shops with money provided by remittances. Several women with family overseas spoke to

---

[55] Cubans' use of the verb *ganar* to describe acquiring goods is telling as in Spanish *ganar* means both "to earn" and "to win." The phrase therefore perfectly expresses the way in which socialist consumption is popularly conceived in Cuba: Consumer goods seem to arrive more by chance than by hard work or a steady accumulation of savings, and distribution is seen to be subject to the whims of invisible state officials.

me of the difficulties returnees face in bringing valuable goods through customs. Concern about having items confiscated is ever-present. Tourists traveling to Cuba also face the scrutiny of customs officers; male tourists may be questioned over women's clothes in their suitcases, and large amounts of clothing or appliances may be treated with suspicion. To avoid such situations, some members of the diaspora prefer to send or bring money and buy goods for relatives in the expensive Cuban shops (*la shopping*).

For larger goods such as appliances and furniture, it is almost inconceivable that the expensive dollar-shop prices are affordable without the support of remittances from the Cuban diaspora. An informal economy of carpenters and tradespeople are the common source of larger furnishings. Dollar shops are seen as extortionate not only for their high prices, but also for the poor quality of the goods. The workmanship of local tradespeople is often more trusted than imported dollar-shop alternatives for household furniture. The relatively low value of Cuban pesos and inexpensive local labor make independently produced furniture such as dining sets affordable for many residents. Thus, the remittance economy fuels the livelihoods of many Cubans who do not receive money from abroad but whose skills and services are largely used by those who do. Tomasito is just one example of such a person. Although he has an official job as a government laborer, which provides him with some useful benefits and resources along with the modest salary, Tomasito gains a larger part of his income from odd jobs, carpentry and house painting. Tomasito's main clients are nearby residents who regularly receive foreign currency by renting rooms to tourists or from children living abroad.

But for consumer goods that require a high level of manufacturing – and the clearest examples are electronic appliances – *la shopping* has, since the early 1990s, been the only legal place to buy these, although an informal market of selling and repairing manufactured goods also exists. To buy smaller appliances such as electric fans or blenders in *la shopping*, Cubans often pay the equivalent of two or three months' salary. Given that even basic necessities (such as soap, oil or toothpaste) require more than the average monthly salary, saving up for such items from an official Cuban salary is virtually impossible. Instead, people must rely on money from relatives or friends abroad, or must cultivate relations (whether business, friendship or romantic) with people in Cuba who can provide them with U.S. dollars or Euros. Typically, these people are foreigners, Cubans working in industries related to tourism, or high-level professionals whose work provides opportunities for travel and/or productivity bonuses in convertible pesos (CUC).

Mapping dollar-shop goods and gifts from abroad provides insight into the social impact of remittance economies that supplement the macro-economic methods used to measure the heightened significance that remittances have assumed (Pérez-López & Diaz-Briquets 2005:396-409). Measuring remittances is particularly hard in Cuba because the government does not disaggregate remittance incomes in economic statistics, and because of restrictions on Cuban-American remittances and the hefty charges for official transfers, a number of remittances come by unofficial ways that are hard to capture. Although the United Nations Economic Commission for Latin America and the Caribbean (ECLAC) estimates that in 2003 US$ 900 million were sent to Cuba from residents in the United States, other estimates vary from US$ 400 to US$ 800 million a year (Pérez-López & Diaz-Briquets 2005:396-409). An alternative method to understand the central role of remittances is to consider their impact on the material lives of individuals and households. In this way, a material culture approach offers a methodological advantage to understanding economic change within Cuba. Although few Cubans will openly disclose the amount of money they receive in addition to their official pensions and salaries, most (if not all) are happy to discuss the paths by which consumer goods and domestic items have made their way into their houses – and people are even happier to speculate about the material riches that are being enjoyed by their neighbors!

Another category of domestic material culture is keeping or recycling goods produced before the revolution. Some categories of domestic goods, such as picture frames, which were not essential items during the Soviet period, have effectively been unavailable for purchase since the 1960s.

Similarly, floor tiles – a key architectural feature of Cuban design from the 1800s until the 1950s – became essentially unavailable as the priorities of the Cuban economy shifted according to the tenets of socialism. As a result many of the goods Cubans use in their houses today are the same objects that their parents or grandparents used before the revolution.

Fig. 13 *Living room furnishings*

This is especially the case in houses that were occupied by bourgeois families; generations' worth of accumulated dressers, rocking chairs, crystal ware and antiques became even more valuable assets because of limited opportunities to acquire domestic commodities.

Elisabeth's living room is an example of the degree to which pre-revolutionary material culture is of ongoing use and importance. Since Elisabeth moved into her current house in the 1980s, she has bought very few items of furniture or decoration; virtually all her living room furniture, and most furniture in other parts of the house, dates from before the revolution. The elderly woman with whom Elisabeth's family shared the house until her death married into a family that had occupied it at least since the end of the nineteenth century, and much of the household furniture was acquired during the early years of her marriage. In one corner of Elisabeth's living room is a glass-fronted art deco cabinet, filled with crystal and ceramics. According to Elisabeth, most of the contents date from the 1940s. She told me, "There's nothing from the dollar shop there. It's all from before." On the wall is a large railway clock that was given to the old woman's father-in-law as a retirement gift. One day as I was admiring this clock, the old woman told me it had been made in the year of her birth, 1918. Effectively, for 45 years Elisabeth's elderly charge lived with the domestic material inheritance that she had accrued by the beginning of the revolution. Although her circumstances were greatly reduced, the remaining assets of the old woman's house indicate how pre-revolutionary wealth, class and race have continued to differentiate the living conditions of families today. Despite a considerable loss in social and financial capital since the "triumph of the revolution," the post-bourgeoisie of Santiago de Cuba frequently retain not only educational and racial advantages, but also a significant (albeit reduced) proportion of material property, which increases their chances of a sustainable domestic economy. The theme of struggle, therefore, as personified by the Cubans who overcame their poverty through the revolution, can be seen to have a counterpoint in the dichotomous moral order by which maintaining the status and cultural capital acquired before the revolution can improve one's chances of living respectably according to the tenets of contemporary socialism.

The continuing usefulness of bourgeois relics is an important reminder of the engagement of middle-class Cubans with globalized (or Americanized) consumer culture well before the revolution. As outlined in the Introduction, kitchens were a particularly potent symbol of "American" technology and modernity for Europeans in the Cold War years (Oldenziel & Zachmann 2009). But for Cubans in the first year of revolution, but not yet communist, American kitchen appliances were never imbued with ideological dangers. The goods I refer to as bourgeois relics are appreciated for the comforts they offer but although they manifest the material resources that pre-revolutionary wealth can continue to provide, they are by no means equated with political identification with the United States. The familiarity of the average urban Cuban with modern consumer culture was not reduced but reinforced by the high socialism of the 1970s to the late 1980s when the Cuban government promoted the value of key consumer commodities in homes. Perhaps the most important scheme for the acquisition of key domestic items in this period was known as Plan CTC, named after the *Central de Trabajadores de Cuba* or Cuban Workers Federation. Under this scheme workers could gain merit points through exemplary conduct and extra productivity, which resulted in a voucher to buy large domestic items. Specific shops in Santiago de Cuba were assigned to stock these goods, and workers could choose an item equal to the value of their voucher. Typical examples of items obtained via Plan CTC that are still used include sewing machines, refrigerators, irons and radios.

For women such as Fernanda, and to a lesser extent Nilda, the socialist voucher system had an impact on their domestic space that is significant to this day. Nilda's salary is one of the highest possible peso salaries, and in the early years of her marriage (from 1976 to 1990), she and her husband could comfortably provide for their family with their two professional salaries. While interviewing Nilda, I asked her to date the various items that were in one room of her house – in this case, her bedroom. None of the items dated from before the revolution and only one object was less than 10 years old, a digital clock sent by Nilda's brother in Miami. Every other piece of furniture in the room arrived in Nilda's house between the late 1970s and late 1980s. Her bed and wardrobe were bought in Cuban pesos, and her television and refrigerator were earned through Plan CTC. Many other items in Nilda's house were bought through voucher systems; for example, in 1978, when Nilda was pregnant with Sonia, she and her mother took turns in a three-day queue for an electric fan that is still used in the house. Mementos from holidays, a modest library and most of Nilda's kitchenware are testament to the fact that Nilda's peak period of acquiring household furniture coincided with the peak of the socialist shop system and the peak of her salary in real terms. In short, the prosperity and respect that professional salary-earners enjoyed in the Soviet period are still reflected in the contemporary material culture of homes like Nilda's. In Fernanda's house few of her appliances or furniture items were bought without voucher schemes or worker benefits. Fernanda's involvement in community organizations, and her husband's diligence in the workplace, allowed them opportunities to "earn" (*ganar*) important domestic goods. In addition to the refrigerator, fan, radio and iron that Fernanda's husband earned through Plan CTC, other perks of his workplace included the ability to purchase linens and other household items at subsidized prices.

Nilda and Fernanda prospered through their identity as socialist citizens: Nilda as a worker and Fernanda as a community leader. Their ability and interest in advancing the work of the revolution allowed them to prosper materially in the decades they were most devoted to their homes. In the 1970s Fernanda had young children and a husband in the mid-career; in the 1980s Nilda was in a similar stage. Consequently, many of their domestic material investments were the result of Soviet-period consumption policies. A striking comparison can be made between the living rooms of Fernanda and Nilda with that of Reina, as Reina has not had opportunities to acquire goods through Plan CTC or similar schemes. Therefore, despite the equalizing goals of the housing and salary reforms of the Cuban revolution, these policies have reinforced the tremendous importance that inheritance plays in determining the character and quality of domestic life in contemporary Cuba. Although the lack of inherited goods was ameliorated through participation in socialist schemes and institutions, the material household legacy acquired in capitalist or Soviet years is a most important factor in differentiating the living standards of neighbors in Santiago de Cuba.

This brief overview suggests that, despite the ideological opposition of socialism and capitalism in public and political rhetoric, such distinctions are not important in the material culture of everyday life. Rather, people try to patch together and acquire as many capitalist, socialist and post-Soviet goods as possible according to their diverse circumstances and histories.[56] There is nothing unusual in Cuba about finding staunch socialists who rave about the superior quality of Westinghouse fridges and people who quietly disengage from or are openly frustrated with state socialism boast of the durability of their Russian blenders and air-conditioners. We can see even from these brief examples how available material goods and the people who can acquire them have shaped domestic interiors over the years. But across all material changes a continuing cultural project has been the acquisition and display of living room.

---

[56] This is a very different perspective to that found in much other anthropological literature on socialist and postsocialist consumption, particularly in Europe. See for example Berdahl, D. 1999. *Where the World Ended: Re-unification and Identity in the German Borderland.* Berkeley: University of California Press; Humphrey, C. 1995. "Creating a Culture of Disillusionment: Consumption in Moscow, a Chronicle of Changing Times." In Miller, D (Ed.) *Worlds Apart: Modernity Through the Prism of the Local.* London and New York: Routledge, pp. 43-68.

goods. The living room, although seemingly a neutral space where people are free to operate with minimal reference to ideology, gender or public status, is actually a zone for negotiating the complex tensions of contemporary politics and morality Through organizing their domestic spaces, women are invoking social and political meanings with reference to the histories and relationships that extend beyond the doorsteps of their houses to other parts of the city and world.

The "biographies" of the things to be found in the living rooms of Santiago are clues to broader structures of production, distribution and consumption (Kopytoff 1988). The goods found in these living rooms – whether from abroad; Soviet technologies; bourgeois, Christian or socialist relics; rugs from the Middle East; medals won in Angola; digital clocks brought from Miami or electric fans made in China – trace a history of global politics and economics that runs much deeper than the nationalist-isolationist rhetoric of the state, and is countered by Cubans with dreams of abroad (*el extranjero*). Cuban women creatively appropriate the diverse materials that constitute their domestic spaces in complex and sometimes contradictory ways. The lack of control over the production and distribution of such goods in no way diminishes interest in practices of active consumption (Miller 1987). On the contrary, as citizens who feel frustrated by and deprived of opportunities for consumption, Cubans seek commodities with which to build, furnish and decorate their homes with a fervor and energy that might outstrip that in he so-called consumerist societies of the capitalist West.

Fig. 14 *An inventive re-use of household goods*

Arguments presented in earlier sections of this book, about the prevailing sense of scarcity that defines contemporary Cuba, might seem odd because the women I worked with all have houses with concrete roofs, televisions, refrigerators and, in some cases, cabinets full of glassware, antique clocks, DVD players and computers. But Cuba's particular history – not only in a longstanding orientation toward mass consumption during its capitalist years, but also envisioning a socialist future in which life is materially better – along with the reality that the material culture of the outside world is largely glimpsed through the second-hand stories of emigrants, imported television shows or through the antics of foreign visitors on vacation – reinforces the sense of injustice that Cubans feel in not being able to enjoy the material security that they understand to be a right of citizenship (Porter 2008). Unlike societies in which opportunities for consumption are seen as stable or improving, in contemporary Cuba it is the experience of material scarcity that drives approaches to home decoration and renovation and that justifies the indefatigable energy that women pour into improving the material and aesthetic standards of their house. Making a similar point, Daphne Berdahl's study of consumption in a village on the East German border argues that before and after the fall of the Berlin wall consumption was a key arena for the demonstration of social difference. The disappearance of the old elites and reduced opportunities for distinction between residents by other means placed a greater emphasis on consumption – and on the social capital of connections that enabled consumption – as a means of asserting social status. For Berdahl, it was the "economy of shortages" experienced under socialism that created a cultural order in which social networks and the possession of consumer goods were greatly prized (Berdahl 1999:118). The second half of this chapter is a closer examination of two prized consumer goods, the refrigerator and electric fan, in which political and economic policies intersect with the intimate experiences of home and family.

Consuming Technologies: Domestic Appliances and the 2006 Energy Revolution

During research in 2006, daily conversation in Santiago was full of discussion about electric appliances. When I asked women in the Tivolí what changes the previous year had brought, almost all began a litany of the effects of the *Año de la Revolución Energética,* or Year of the Energy Revolution. Fidel Castro and his ministers proclaimed 2006 as the year to resolve the energy crises plaguing Cuba as the old Soviet-era energy infrastructure, prohibitive petrol prices and bad weather translated to water and power shortages across the country (Economist Intelligence Unit 2006:19-23). With the benefit of favorable trade and investment with Canada, Norway, India, China and Venezuela, the Cuban government began repairing power plants, securing water supplies and, particularly important, reducing energy use (Economist Intelligence Unit 2006:22-3). To reduce domestic energy use, the government acted on two fronts: first to significantly increase the price of electricity and second to replace old domestic appliances with newer, energy-efficient models. For each old television or refrigerator in the house, citizens were encouraged to buy replacements imported from China, with the option of payments over time. The Soviet refrigerators and black-and-white televisions that were mainstays of the

Tivolí houses in 2004 had been replaced by updated Chinese models.[57] In addition to large appliances, each household was allocated electric cooking appliances to offset the end of the supply of liquid gas with which most families cooked. Thus, by the time of my visit, each kitchen in Santiago de Cuba had recently acquired an identical electric hotplate, rice cooker, "multipurpose" pressure cooker and portable water heater.

Although purchasing these goods was not compulsory, all of the women I spoke to had bought their appliances as soon as possible to cope with the change from gas and to lessen the increase in their electricity bills.

And so, as these changes were news at the time of my trip, each visit to a household in the Tivolí was full of questions, rumors, complaints and jokes about the new domestic technologies. Several of my informants were eager to explain the changes and were quick to recount rumors of future replacements and recite the prices they had paid for each new item.

> *Dominga*: And so, they've been changing all of these things; they changed the televisions, and they're giving circuit breakers....Now we don't use the liquid gas to cook, they gave out hotplates and also those cookers – over at your house, didn't they give those out too?

---

[57] The biographies of domestic interiors discussed earlier in this chapter continue to manifest the changing global political landscapes that affect Cuban consumption, as Chinese appliances have increasingly been added to kitchens that feature legacies of previous periods such as American crockery and Soviet blenders.

Anna: Yes, those are the famous "multipurpose" cookers, aren't they?

Dominga: Yes, that's right. And they are also substituting the water heaters, and the rice cookers. The social workers have the job of coming and checking that you have all the right things, because look, for example they will exchange the broken electric fans (for new ones), but those big refrigerators, if they're broken, they won't exchange them. Soon they're also going to change all the washing machines. They say they will be giving out eleven items in total, and so far they've given about five or six of them.

As with all changes, some people were happier than others. Odalys, for example, was very pleased with her new refrigerator when I visited her, as it had more freezer space than the Soviet model she previously owned. For some residents, the changes of the Year of the Energy Revolution were bringing unexpected opportunities: Fernanda's granddaughter had been deployed to Havana for a month to work on domestic inventories of electronic goods, enjoying her stay very much. One of their neighbors was taking advantage of the exchange system to replace two broken televisions to send to her son in Havana. However, despite the improvements that these aspects of the government plan brought, most of the women I spoke to felt that these changes had a negative effect on their lives. Some women resented having to change from gas cooking, while others were worried about the prices of the new consumer goods they felt obliged to buy. Stories were circulating about water heaters breaking after two weeks of use, and people complained that relying on electricity to cook would mean that people would be left without food to eat during power cuts. Because these adjustments to the routines of domestic life were affecting every household of Santiago de Cuba, it is not surprising that these additions to everybody's living room and kitchen were the prevailing subject of conversation among the women of the Tivolí.

The energy revolution is one of many examples of how connected state policy and domestic life remain in Cuba. The exchange system instituted for the Year of the Energy Revolution had in a few short months transformed the material culture of Cuban homes, changing how people cook, bathe and sleep, altering their short-term savings plans and dominating community life and everyday conversations. Despite the expectations in much literature on Cuba of the mid-1990s that the Cuban state had begun an inevitable "transition" to capitalism (for example, see Córdova 1996; Kildegaard & Orro Fernández 1999), by 2006 it had become clear that despite (or more precisely because of) the economic reforms of the Special Period, the state remains central in providing and distributing goods to the population, and is of particular importance to citizens who lack access to foreign currency.

More interesting, the changes of 2006 are evidence that both government policymakers and Cuban citizens were aware of the significance of domestic technologies and the relationship of domestic material culture to the ongoing legitimacy of the Cuban revolution. Although the Year of the Energy Revolution incorporated broader reforms, such as the decentralization of power generation and investment in new energy sources, the only aspects of the program that interested people in the Tivolí were the rising cost of electricity and the new appliances. Domestic appliances are highly valued in contemporary Cuba, and although they are sometimes taken for granted, their anchoring of daily life means that their importance is most realized when not having them seems a distinct possibility (Miller 1998a:3-21). Particularly for women (but also for men), the difference between having and not having a refrigerator or electric fan can transform their life in practical and intangible ways. "Modern" appliances and media technologies in the home[58] can be understood as objects loaded with personal, social and political significance related to the functional impact that such objects have upon women's lives and relationships.

It is usually in struggles over domestic technologies that explicit (and sometimes ferocious) socio-political contestations can be found within neighborhoods and between consumers in Cuba. Chapter 3 considered groceries, a category of consumer goods that also matter. It was the very banality of these items that made the difficulty

---

[58] Although I recognize that other tools in the Cuban home also constitute technology, my discussion is restricted to the technologies understood by Cubans to fall within the sphere of "domestic appliances" (*equipos electrodomésticos*). In 2004, the specific appliances considered in a survey I undertook of 40 households were televisions, refrigerators, electric fans, air conditioners, radios, washing machines, video recorders, computers, blenders, CD players and cassette players. To keep the survey as short as possible, other appliances that I judged would not add new aspects to my analysis, such as rice cookers and irons, were excluded.

of their acquisition so outrageous for consumers, as ideas of "normal" grocery acquisition were different from the lived experience of battling for them. However, the battles over the domestic appliances considered in this chapter suggest that these are different from the everyday struggles of consumption considered earlier. Objects such as refrigerators are treated as serious investments loaded with practical and symbolic meaning. Whereas the battle to consume groceries is enacted through daily short-term sacrifices such as queuing in the afternoon sun, scrubbing potatoes, and watering down detergent to make it last longer, strategies to acquire and maintain the domestic appliances discussed here and in the next chapter require sacrifices and plans over a longer period of time. Domestic technologies such as refrigerators and electric fans are major investments and have become more expensive in the post-Soviet era.[59] Working to obtain these goods remains difficult, and the effort of acquiring new domestic technologies, whether through saving money or cultivating relationships (and most often through a combination of both), is demonstrated in the tension and anxiety with

---

[59] In 1988 Rosendahl listed the following appliances as available in shops but prohibitively expensive: electric fan 90 to 120 pesos, refrigerator 700 to 1000 pesos, TV 500 to 600 pesos. (Rosendahl 1997:37). Many of the items acquired were not actually bought at these prices, as earning goods through Plan CTC would substantially reduce their prices, so that a fan with a retail price of 90 pesos would, for example, be bought through Plan CTC at 40 pesos. By 2004 in contrast, an electric fan cost the equivalent of 625 pesos (US $25), a refrigerator 12,500 pesos and a television 8,750 pesos. Even the prices of subsidized Chinese goods for sale in 2006 were substantially higher in proportion to official incomes than those sold in the Soviet period.

which changes to domestic technologies are treated by women in the Tivolí. To appreciate how important obtaining a new refrigerator was to Cubans in 2006, it is worth considering how much refrigerators were a topic of discussion and concern in my 2004 field research, even before the schemes of the Year of the Energy Revolution.

In 2004, Elisabeth was preoccupied with the state of her refrigerator, which seemed to be on the verge of collapse and was already creating extra domestic labor as a result:

> *Anna*: Which domestic appliance was the hardest to acquire?
>
> *Elisabeth*: For the price? The fridge. Five hundred sixty dollars. It's not easy. We have to raise a lot of pigs, to be able to achieve this. That's why we try… in dollars, I think it's 70 dollars, or 90 dollars, not more…to fix the fridge. They have fixed the motor; my husband fixed it somewhat so it more or less keeps cold. But we can't put anything in the freezer. The chicken, we have to store with friends, or with family. The fish we salt, to preserve it.

In the short survey I conducted of 40 Tivolí households in 2004, 5 contained refrigerators that predated the Cuban revolution. A larger number of residents, including Nilda and Fernanda, acquired their refrigerators in the Soviet period through workplace and other distribution schemes. The family refrigerator was the single most expensive material investment of most households in this study.[60] The

---

[60] Cars are more expensive than refrigerators, but none of the respondents I worked with owned cars. Nilda's ex-husband had bought

prospect of having to buy a new refrigerator was acknowledged by several of my informants as a source of considerable anxiety:

> *Anna:* What is generally the most difficult appliance to acquire?

> *Nilda*: Most difficult? The refrigerators, for their price.

> *Anna*: And how did you come to have the two refrigerators in this house?

> *Nilda*: One, in Cuban pesos, which my brother bought for my mother. And the other was earned by my husband in his workplace. We paid for it in installments. That was quite a while ago.

> *Anna*: What was the hardest appliance to acquire in this house?

> *Fernanda*: The fridge.

> *Anna:* The fridge was difficult [to acquire]?

> *Fernanda:* No. No, my husband earned it, at work. And the television I earned myself, through the CDR. But what I mean to say is, if we had had to buy them in the street, it would have been very difficult. Because they cost a lot, they're very expensive.

---

her children a computer, which cost more than their refrigerator bought in the late 1980s. However, Nilda's household was one of only two in my study that had a home computer. The other household had recently bought a new refrigerator that cost more than their computer. The physician daughter who lives in Europe financed both items.

If a consumer had to resort to purchasing a refrigerator, whether officially in a dollar store or unofficially second-hand from another household, the cost was high. A refrigerator retailing at US $500 in the dollar shop can only be bought with the assistance of remittances or with extended dollar income through a small business or tourism-related work. Nevertheless, a total of six refrigerators in my survey had been bought in local dollar shops, again suggesting that (as with the media technologies discussed in Chapter 5) despite the lack of income for everyday goods, ways are found to invest in crucial technologies definitive of a modern home. In her study of the production and consumption of refrigerators in postwar United States, historian Shelley Nickles suggests that refrigerators were so compelling because they "embodied a modernity that reflected a logic based in the household: consumption of new technology and style, but also thrift, efficiency, cleanliness, convenience and flexibility" (Nickles 2002b:723). My research in the Tivolí suggests that very similar expectations of a modern domestic space were developed in Cuba in the course of the twentieth century. However, a major difference between consumers in the postwar United States and consumers in post-Soviet Cuba is that although twentieth-century capitalism encouraged U.S. housewives to choose from an ever-greater variety of increasingly affordable refrigerators (Nickles 2002a: 582-585), the economic transformation of the Special Period left Cuban housewives with a deep need for household refrigerators without the resources to afford or maintain them.

To live without a refrigerator, or with one that is not fully functional as Elisabeth described, is a source of stress and unwelcome work. Women in the Tivolí were quick to acknowledge the importance of a refrigerator in their domestic routines. The preservation of food in turn allowed women considerable preservation of their own time and labor. When explaining why she felt her refrigerator to be her most important possession, Reina exclaimed, "If my fridge were to break down, I …oh my gosh, I would die!" In Yanet's house in 2004, the refrigerator broke down a few weeks after she and her mother had bought a new video recorder, and Yanet told me ruefully that if they had known that their refrigerator was on the verge of breaking down they would have saved their money instead for the necessary repairs. Yanet's mother explained to me that after her refrigerator broke down she had to go to the market almost every day after work as she could not store meat or other perishable products in her kitchen. A neighbor allowed her to store some of her rationed perishable foods in her refrigerator, but Yanet's mother said that the situation embarrassed her as she had to ask permission to collect her food and did not have the freedom to enter the neighbor's house at odd hours. She was also embarrassed because she could not offer guests a glass of chilled water, or make chilled soft drinks for Yanet to enjoy in the afternoon after work.

Refrigerators offer the possibility of time-shifting, a concept more often explored with reference to media technologies (Gray 1992). The capacity to temporally reorder domestic routines enhances women's domestic lives in meaningful ways, especially because women's public lives in Cuba are frequently characterized by coping with obstacles such as shopping queues, workplace meetings, slow public transport, doctors' appointments and children's schooling. The irregularity of fresh food supplies forces women to buy meat and fish when they have the opportunity and make them last as long as possible. For example, fish allocated via basic rations arrives at the *carnicería* monthly, and, particularly for households whose extra sources of protein are limited, it is vital to be able to freeze fish for later. Working women rely on refrigerators to store food in order to best use their limited time for cooking. The refrigerator is one of the few tools in daily life that makes domestic labor more flexible in an overfilled schedule that is largely unpredictable and frequently frustrating.

If refrigerators enable the adjustment of time, then domestic technologies that cool bodies rather than food have an equally important ability to reconstitute space. As Elizabeth Shove suggests in the context of twentieth-century North America, in addition to increasing the number of social interactions that occur within domestic spaces, "air conditioning was also drawing people back out of other social networks" (Shove 2003:44), and Tivolí women identify controlling the indoor climate as important in creating a comfortable home and enhancing the quality of family life. Air conditioning is beyond the economic possibilities of most people in the Tivolí, both for the initial outlay and because of the energy consumption and maintenance costs. However, electric fans are important in domestic life in Santiago, which is commonly thought to be Cuba's hottest city. Although larger old houses (such as

Elisabeth's) may have retained the high ceilings and large windows to allow airflow, the subdivisions, renovations and new constructions have maximized available space at the cost of ventilation. Houses such as Reina's and Yanet's, both of which were adapted over the years, have few windows, low ceilings, and use industrial fittings and materials not conducive to cool interiors. Managing heat indoors is therefore a genuine preoccupation for many women in the Tivolí, and electric fans are high on the wish lists of the women interviewed. Many women reported that they had saved up to buy multiple electric fans, and they connected their concern with creating a comfortable climate to their identity as mothers:

> *Anna:* What is the most recent appliance you acquired for the household?
>
> *Elisabeth*: A fan. When the baby was born. That was in January, early January – eight months ago.
>
> *Anna*: Do you have any plans to buy domestic appliances in the future?
>
> *Elisabeth*: Yes. This little pig, this sow we have now, we want to sell her to buy a fan for the older boy. Because he's in the last bedroom, which is small, and it gets very hot. He doesn't have a fan – well, we have one, but it's very bad, it makes a lot of noise. We want to buy that. We want to buy, we don't have, an iron. Well, we do and we don't have one! We have one of those Russian ones, those ones that came from before, which are very good, but this one just can't be

fixed anymore. We have to buy another one. Um, we want to buy....a video. The fridge, we have to fix it. And it has to be in dollars. In dollars, all of it.

As Elisabeth notes, electric fans increase the comfort of children, in particular helping them to sleep. This concern with comfortable sleeping environments for their children was expressed even more strongly by Reina. One of the few times I felt Reina was openly sad and frustrated by her poverty was in an emotional discussion regarding her desire to buy a fan for her son:

> *Anna:* Are you planning to buy any appliances in the dollar shops?

> *Reina:* No, no way. I can't. Although, the little boy gets too hot. I have one fan, which doesn't rotate, which isn't very good, and I have to battle to buy a fan. I'm going to be honest with you. Sometimes I go out on the street. And although I know that it'll drive me crazy, the little boy, he gives me a kiss and...even if there's people who say to me that I do something to them even if it's just ...to be able to get a fan. Because in this way, well you can imagine. I didn't even have a bed. I bought beds – mine, my dad's and my grandmother's. Think about it. A fan for the little boy is the only thing I need.

In this conversation Reina is ambiguous about the ways in which she makes small amounts of money by going out to the street, but in other conversations it is clear that sex work is one of the strategies she has employed. Reina's struggling to save for an electric fan is indicative of her considerable poverty even by Tivolí standards, as many households managed over time to buy several electric fans in *la shopping* for US $25 to $35. Another elderly resident in my 2004 survey told me that she saved up to buy a fan in the dollar store for her grandson by selling homemade juices for one *peso* a glass until she had saved up enough. We calculated that she must have sold more than 1,000 drinks over a period of approximately four months to buy her grandson's fan. Unfortunately, soon after our conversation her blender broke; as she needed the blender to make the drinks, her small enterprise could not continue, and she was unable to work toward buying further appliances in this way.

As suggested at the beginning of this chapter, socioeconomic differences between residents of the Tivolí, which may not be evident in non-material ways, are mapped by the presence or absence of such key household items as electric fans. Whereas Reina is making do with one fan that was "invented" by her partner from spare parts, Fernanda has been able to add one fan bought in *la shopping* to the several others that she and her husband earned through the Plan CTC, and Nilda's household uses three electric fans that were all bought in *la shopping*. By tracing the use of electric fans it can be seen how women in the Tivolí have drawn upon combinations of social, economic and political capital in their struggles to build comfortable homes. As historians and sociologists have argued with reference to the broader twentieth-century transformation of domestic technologies, refrigerators and electric fans, among other appliances, can be seen in Cuba to be important in constructing appropriate patterns of domesticity that attempt to meet expectations of hygiene, efficiency and comfort. In the very practical ways in which refrigerators and electric fans transform everyday domestic practices, domestic technologies allow people to feel greater control over home life. Ruth Schwartz Cowan has observed that during the twentieth century domestic technologies have brought leisure and labor activities into the home that previously would have been provided through outside services or activities. As a result, the effects of industrialization in the home have not been to reduce overall hours spent on housework, but rather to minimize the drudgery while creating higher expectations of housework encouraged by notions of scientific motherhood (Cowan 1983:42-7). This can certainly be seen in Cuba, where a distinct appeal of the technologies discussed lies in the increased use of the home as a space of both leisure and labor. In combination, domestic technologies minimize drudgery and maximize comfort in the home. Refrigerators also provide temporal control over shopping and cooking, minimizing time at markets and in shop queues, and electric fans create cool comfort in the home instead of spending evenings outdoors. Domestic technologies can also generate income, free women to work outside the home and encourage members of the household to spend an increased amount of time at the home.

In this sense, when women invest in domestic technologies they can be seen to be investing in relationships (Silva 2002; Pahl 1990). Despite the investment required, with domestic technologies Cuban woman are not only enhancing the quality of their domestic experience but also fulfilling their role as providers of sustenance, comfort and hospitality to children, partners, relatives and friends.

The material culture of homes in the Tivolí provides a map of complex and changing social and political status, as well as ethnographic evidence of how domestic technologies have both functional and symbolic power in transforming and representing domestic life. The particular power of domestic technologies—what makes them such important acquisitions—is the ability to control time and space in the domestic realm in the face of economic scarcity, political change and conditions that challenge all women running households. Although in some ways the failures of socialism seem to restrict the ability of Cuban women to achieve desired levels of comfort and convenience in the home, in other ways, such as the schemes of the Year of the Energy Revolution, the state continues to support the longstanding association of womanly virtue with domestic activity through a socialist imagery of modernity that privileges efficiency, hygiene, comfort and convenience. For this reason, for many Cuban women the crises of contemporary life are most problematically manifested in the struggles to maintain domestic routines. After all, as Shelley Nickles notes in her history of American refrigerators, the kitchen (and I would add the home in general) is a space "not only for social aspiration and belonging but also for conflicts over power in the creation of a modern, consumer society" (Nickles 2002b:727).

Chapter 5

If They Show "Prison Break" in the United States on a Wednesday, by Thursday It Is Here: *Television and New Media in Twenty-First Century Cuba*

One of the misconceptions underlying popular discussion about Cuba is that a primary media issue is political censorship. It is certainly true that all telecommunications and media infrastructure in Cuba is state-controlled and that access to such technologies and media is determined by political rather than commercial considerations. Furthermore, much state-produced Cuban media is dedicated to news and current affairs and closely connected to the viewpoints and objectives of the socialist government. Consequently, the socialist newspapers, television and radio broadcasts, and more recent media and communication technologies such as mobile phones and the Internet, have been central and visible platforms upon which the Cold War politics of the U.S. and Cuba have been staged. Significant scholarly attention has been paid to the technology, politics and economics of both the Cuban media industry and the U.S. anti-socialist media initiatives of such organizations as Radio Martí, which has been broadcasting news and political critique in Spanish to Cuba from the United States since 1983, although broadcasts are effectively jammed by Cuba (Ruíz Miyares 1999; Alexandre 1992).

What has been given less attention is the role of television and electronic media in the everyday life of average Cubans, who rely upon Cuban media for their understanding of world and national events, but for whom media consumption is more typically a form of entertainment or escape than a forum for political resistance. In the twenty-first century, Cuban consumers have seen the development of a new media landscape in which state broadcasts have been supplemented by a wider range of entertainment and communication choices than was technologically possible or ideologically tolerated in the Soviet socialist years. Although the Cuban media landscape is in some ways different from its neighbors in the Americas by the absence of commercial media and access to media technologies, there are also ways in which the typical media consumption in Cuba is much the same as anywhere in Latin America. For the most part, people switch on their televisions to enjoy the evening *telenovela*, rent or copy DVDs to watch Hollywood movies and a few also check their email to keep up with faraway friends and family.

Recognizing similarities to other mediascapes is as important as outlining the differences if we want to understand how and why media is such an important dimension of everyday consumption in contemporary Cuba, which is the intention of this chapter. In particular, I examine how the strategies that the Cuban government adopted to deal with traditional or established media such as television differ from those applied to newer media and information technologies. The chapter then discusses how the tactics of invention and circumvention we have seen Cuban consumers employ in other spheres of everyday life are also deployed in their pursuit of electronic entertainment. Indeed, it is the pursuit of such entertainment, much more than an interest in politics, which motivates Cuban media consumption. Finally, I explore how "mobile media" – a phrase of increasing currency in media studies – take unique and specific forms in Cuba and also move technology-enabled sectors of the Cuban community closer to the global circuits of popular culture that dominate the media landscapes of their contemporaries elsewhere in the Americas.

Although all material objects can communicate identities, convey status, trace histories or embody political and economic tensions, the objects and technologies of electronic and digital media such as televisions, mobile phones, computers and zip drives have properties that make them doubly communicative. Few objects in modern societies "speak to us" so literally as do media and communication technologies. Roger Silverstone and Eric Hirsch identify this capacity of media technologies as a "double articulation": both as technological objects and as transmitters of media, they are the domestic technologies by which politics, economics and culture can be most clearly produced, reproduced and contested (Silverstone & Hirsch 1992:1). From 2003, when my fieldwork first documented the role and importance of television, until

2009, when I interviewed young Cubans about their use of portable hard drives to store and circulate copies of international films and television shows, it has been clear to me that understanding media consumption requires analysis not only of the contents of and audience for media, but also of the technological properties that have been transforming the everyday practices of Cubans who have increasing access to media devices.

Perhaps more significant, as detailed below, the unusual political and economic context in which Cubans access media forms and technologies highlights a politics of media that is contrary to my original expectations of Cuba. Consumers only rarely expressed concern about their access to controversial content; they were more concerned about the widening divide between those who have access to electronic media and those who do not. As media and communications technologies have been changing dramatically, the models developed early in the revolution for mass media such as television do not meet the requirements of new media, particularly within the political and economic context of Cuba. What emerges is an interesting world in which Cuban consumers are remarkably current with mainstream media culture in the Latin American-Caribbean region, but their experience of such culture takes place within an unusual infrastructure with distinctive routes for the consumption and circulation of media contents and technologies.

Individual media technologies have enjoyed different degrees of support and distribution in post-revolutionary Cuba. At one end of the spectrum, television and radio have been central to the development of Cuban socialism, with the state using television and radio programming to shape revolutionary communities. In addition to harnessing radio and television broadcasts to further the revolution, the Cuban state actively distributed media technologies to much of the population. Televisions were acknowledged to be important symbolically and practically, as the revolution was literally brought into living rooms through televisions acquired by way of workplace schemes and neighborhood committees. Such acknowledgment is in stark contrast to the limited tolerance of new media technologies outside of work-related activities. There has been intensive investment in telecommunications infrastructure since the 1990s, which suggests that the Cuban government intends to gradually increase nationwide access to new media and communications. However, until April 2008, personal Internet access and personal cell-phone accounts were prohibited for Cuban citizens, although anecdotal evidence suggests a thriving black market has existed in both technologies for some years (Economist Intelligence Unit 2006; Coté 2005; BBC Mundo April 14 2008).

Although this chapter briefly outlines how government policies toward media have changed over the first decade of the millennium, the main purpose is to provide a background for understanding the practices of Cubans as media consumers. The examples of such practices come from a series of visits to Santiago de Cuba in which I focused on aspects of media consumption. Although much of my research on television and VCR usage took place during research in 2003-2004, during visits in 2006, 2008 and 2009 my focus shifted increasingly to the use of DVD players, mobile phones, personal computers and associated technologies.

Television: A Key Tool of the Revolution

Before the revolution in 1959, Cuba had the highest media penetration in Latin America and, by global standards, was among the earliest adopters of radio and television (Hoffmann 2004:183-185). From the 1930s until the 1950s, Havana was a highly influential center of media production, not only developing the first examples of *radionovelas* and *telenovelas*, but also networks of media producers who influenced the television industry across the Hispanic Caribbean (La Pastina et. al 2003; Rivero 2007). Of course, media access in pre-revolutionary Cuba was extremely uneven, centered in Havana and highly concentrated within the predominantly white middle class. In regional and rural areas and among poor communities, which were disproportionately black, illiteracy and poverty prevented regular mass media access. Nonetheless, the Cuban revolution inherited an established media infrastructure and, despite widespread professional migration, there remained an enthusiastic class of Cuban cultural producers in such fields as television, advertising or journalism who worked to create a new socialist television industry for the country (see Hernandez-Reguant 2002). From 1962, media production was centralized in state institutes (first *Instituto Cubano de Radiodifusión*, later renamed *Instituto Cubano de Radio y Televisión* or ICRT), and the 1976 Constitution prohibits any private mass communication (Hoffmann 2004:183-4). But just as important as centralized television programming were the various community and workplace schemes that included televisions among the consumer goods awarded on the basis of merit or need. Cuban ownership of televisions increased steadily over the second half of the twentieth century.[61]

Delivering film and television to the entire population was an important step toward consolidating a national community not only with a revolutionary consciousness, but also with an understanding of and identification with Cuban culture, as well as a degree of electronic literacy that was unquestionably a hallmark of modernity.[62] My informants recall that even in poorer households, by the early to mid-1970s, televisions were a mainstay of domestic life, particularly in urban areas. A mix of telenovelas, films, news and current affairs, children's programming, sports broadcasts and variety shows with an

---

[61] International Telecommunications Union data shows that the percentage of televisions per 100 people had increased by 100% between 1960 and 1980. In 1965 there were fewer than 5 televisions per 100 people (not in itself a low figure internationally), and by 200 there were 23 per 100 people.

[62] The consciousness with which media access delivered modernity is very nicely portrayed in the 1967 short documentary *Por Primera Vez,* in which traveling projectionists are sent by *ICAIC* to show rural farmers in Guantánamo, the province that borders Santiago de Cuba, a film for the first time. The film they screen is the Charlie Chaplin classic *Modern Times,* and the film audience is watched by us, the documentary audience, being introduced to the wonders of modern entertainment thanks to the Cuban revolution.

emphasis on music and dance has long been the typical fare of Cuban television schedules. Imported programming constituted a large part of television content throughout this period; telenovelas, films, and children's programs in particular included foreign imports. In the 1970s and 1980s, there were a substantial number of programs from the USSR and eastern Europe, but even during this period there was what might be considered as capitalist media content on Cuban television.[63] My Cuban friends and informants who were children in the 1970s and 1980s recall not only a wide range of Russian cartoons, but also children's series from the United Kingdom and Australia, which had been co-produced or dubbed by Spanish production companies. Similarly, telenovelas from Brazil have been avidly followed by Cuban viewers since the 1980s, and anthropologist Mona Rosendahl reports from her ethnographic fieldwork during that period that the Hollywood-produced *Jaws* was a most popular film (1997: 122). As in many other facets of their everyday lives, Cubans have long been involved in transnational circuits of production and consumption of media, even though particular cultural products at particular times may have been marginalized or prohibited by the state. Compared with their counterparts elsewhere in the Caribbean and Latin America, Cubans have on average not been behind in television consumption, and among the urban and rural

---

[63] A well-known study of imported television conducted by Tapio Varis in 69 countries in 1973 and 1983 included an analysis of Cuban television programming (1984). During this period, Cuba imported 20% of its programs from the United States and 19% from the Soviet Union, while programs from the German Democratic Republic and the United Kingdom featured heavily during primetime.

poor, access to television significantly preceded that of equivalent communities.

A story that was related to me shows how valuable televisions continue to be, as perhaps the most sought-after commodity in urban Cuba. One day, while I was visiting Sonia and Nilda's house, I asked Sonia about her neighbors and the relations between the residents of her street. Sonia told me a story of a neighborly dispute that had the whole street talking: Arguments had erupted in their block over the allocation of a new "Panda" Chinese television that had been supplied to their block's CDR (revolutionary committee). My field notes written on the day of Sonia's story reveal a complex web of neighborhood relations full of disputes, envy, allegiances and scandal:

> Silvita, who lives in the same block as Sonia and Nilda, has a reputation for being *bretera* (gossipy) and *problematica* (a troublemaker). At the time of the allocation of the Panda TV she started arguing with her neighbour Mateo as they each thought they should get the television; they stopped talking as a result of the dispute. Silvita normally doesn't involve Nilda's household in her problems, but this time she stopped talking to Nilda for over a month because she believed that Nilda had supported Mateo's claim to the television.

> In the end neither Silvita nor Mateo got the television. It was awarded to another neighbor, Conchita, because she donates blood regularly.

People on the block gossiped that Conchita also slept with the president of the *CDR* to get the television; certainly, Conchita had danced very provocatively with him at a block party around that time. The president of the *CDR* had only recently moved to the block and, although none of the neighbors knew him well, he had assumed the role very quickly. Sonia told me that she finds him very pedantic and distasteful.

Sonia's brother Nikolai had a different opinion of how Conchita was awarded the television; he asserted that Conchita claimed that her daughter is mentally ill and that the state gives priority to people with problems like these. Nikolai also said that he believes Conchita has more mental problems than her supposedly mentally ill daughter!

Sonia took great delight in elaborating the multiple ways in which Tivolí residents employ non-monetary resources to acquire important goods. Socialist distribution schemes may no longer be the primary way consumer goods are acquired, but when such opportunities do arise, one can draw upon the social capital developed through neighborly relations of mutual trust or as faithful workers and committed revolutionaries. The story also provides examples of how bodies can be deployed – through sexual relationships or as medicalized subjects – in exchange for a greater chance of accessing expensive goods.

The residents of Sonia and Nilda's block negotiated and appropriated the formal structures of the CDR with informal and extra-revolutionary strategies. It is when the potential prize is as valuable as a television that the gloves really come off in community disputes; old allegations are rehashed and previously overlooked illegalities denounced. Sonia's account is an example of how television, central to everyday life in urban Cuba, is actively encouraged by the state; televisions are evidently prized objects worth fighting over. They are not, however, particularly rare. The vast majority of households in cities such as Santiago de Cuba own at least one television; in 2004, I surveyed 40 households in the neighborhood of the Tivolí and found a total of 41 functioning televisions. Of those, a majority were acquired during or after the Soviet period, one quarter of them through state distribution programs such as Plan CTC, workplace allocation programs or through occasional neighborhood distribution programs like the one in Sonia's story. Fernanda was allocated her television because of her longstanding involvement in the neighborhood committees of the CDR and the FMC and, as outlined in the previous chapter, workplace or community distribution schemes accounted for most of the major domestic appliances in her household. But households like Fernanda's are no longer typical, and since the partial opening of the economy in the 1990s, increasing numbers of Cubans have found ways to purchase televisions or have them bought by friends or family abroad. Although emigrant remittances have long been key in enabling some households to improve their standard of living (especially since the Special Period), there has been a marked and rapid increase in the ability of Cubans with foreign currency or Cuban Convertible Pesos (CUC) to purchase new televisions and DVD recorders, sound systems, personal computers and mobile phones.

Nilda's household demonstrates how a slow but steady path of upward mobility can be mapped by increasing technological wealth. As outlined in the previous chapter, Nilda had a relatively well-equipped house in 2004 because her ex-husband's employment as a manager at a state enterprise offered productivity bonuses in CUC, as well as opportunities for limited travel abroad. For example Nilda's children had two stereos bought for them in Canada and Mexico by their father, where, she explained, such things are much cheaper than in Cuban stores or on the black market. In 2004, Nilda could not think of any new media technologies that her family specifically wanted, but when I returned to her house in 2006, I found that they had a newer, larger television and that their VCR had been replaced by a DVD player. Nilda had inherited these from her cousin, who had left Cuba and migrated to the United States. Although her cousin's house had been reclaimed by the state, he had managed to pass on his more valuable appliances to Nilda before leaving the country. By 2008, Nilda's material circumstances had improved yet again: her adult son had migrated to Mexico, and he had paid for a new computer and Internet connection so that they could keep in touch. He had also bought her a cell phone so that she could text him in an emergency, and he paid for it from Mexico. Although Nilda's material comforts are by no means ostentatious, she represents the best-case scenario for professional and educated Cubans who have managed to convert their cultural capital, if not into highly paid employment, into favorable working conditions that maximize opportunities for income and/or remittances. Her ex-husband's successful career shows that labor can still yield material advantages in certain areas or industries but, just as important, her family's educational level meant that they were well-placed to migrate abroad and to prosper within a few years of resettlement. Over the same period in which many Cubans who migrated during the 1990s were achieving economic stability abroad and able to send regular remittances home, the prices of consumer electronics were steadily dropping. The increasing affordability of technologies to copy and share media content has been crucial in transforming the media landscape in Cuba. Nilda and her family have changed their consumption habits from watching their Russian television to getting a larger Chinese model and increasingly supplementing their television viewing with films or television shows first on VCR and then on DVD, and more recently by adding e-mail and Internet chat to their regular activities.

But television remains the first step in a domestic media environment such as that now found in Nilda's house, and for the majority of my informants, television remained the main source of news and entertainment, although a growing minority had DVD players. Although new televisions cost from US $350 to $500 in 2004, 17 of the 41 televisions in my study had been bought at the dollar store (*la shopping*). The many dollar purchases of televisions is representative of a paradox of contemporary Cuban consumption: prices are high, commodities are in short supply, people lack income and must plan carefully for small purchases, yet high-cost high-prestige items such as televisions are common in urban households. The rate of VCR ownership in 2004 seemed an even clearer example of this apparent paradox, as 9 of the 40 households had VCRs, a high proportion given the complexity of purchasing a VCR in Cuba and their starting price of US $250. Among other things, the prevalence of televisions bought in dollars suggests that those Cubans who receive regular remittances or foreign-currency earnings simply must acquire more dollars than are officially reported (or unofficially disclosed), as the cost of a television represents more than the annual salaries of a typical household in Santiago de Cuba in 2004.[64]

Many would-be media consumers lack both the dollars to buy new televisions and the revolutionary credentials to be allocated one. Before the Energy Revolution of 2006 offered opportunities to trade in televisions for newer models, people relied on old televisions that had been repaired many times, or bought them second hand on "the street," usually in Cuban pesos. Reina acquired her television this way, as she could never afford a new set. In 2004, just a few months before I met her, she asked around the neighborhood to see if anyone wanted to sell an older model. Reina paid a neighbor in pesos for a medium-sized black-and-white television made in the 1980s. A few months after buying it, the television was malfunctioning and Reina's partner was trying to fix it. As Reina had left the Tivolí when I next returned to visit, I do not know

---

[64] A household that comprised two low to average workers' wages and one pension could average 600 Cuban pesos official income a month. A household with two young professionals' salaries would be similar. Thus, the annual total official income of the household would total $288 a year. Even accounting for free health care, basic rations and other benefits, it is simply impossible to save for a $350 television from such an income.

whether she took part in the Energy Revolution program to acquire a new television in 2006. However, in revisiting other households included in my 2004 study, I found that those who had upgraded their televisions without the Energy Revolution scheme had been able to do so only with financial support from friends or family abroad. Indeed, the households that in 2004 had bought televisions in recent years, and who had VCRs, had by 2009 mostly managed to acquire a DVD player, and in several cases a computer. Households in 2004 that did not have new televisions or VCRs were typically in the same situation by 2009; they had replaced some older appliances with newer models through the Energy Revolution, but had not acquired new *kinds* of domestic technologies. Although this is not rigorous data, my occasional follow-up of these households over a five-year period does seem to reveal a widening gap in Santiago de Cuba, in which increasingly mediated lifestyles are experienced by a small sector of people in the community who have the required economic means, technological knowledge and social networks.

DVD players began to take over VCR technology in Santiago de Cuba between 2005 and 2006, considerably later than in most of the rest of the world. By 2008 and 2009, VCR recorders were rarely in use, as parts to repair them became scarcer and DVD players became cheaper and easier to find. In this section I consider these two technologies together, because both fulfilled the same two functions for Cuban media consumers. First, they offered the possibility of "time-shifting" television viewing, which has been documented by media scholars as significant and holds a particular appeal in the context of Cuba (Pertierra

2008). Second, the copying of films and television programs have allowed an informal economy to flourish in which content is exchanged, gifted, rented and sold.

If television technology represents the triumph of the Cuban revolution, then videocassette recorders and disc players can be seen to represent the disparities and opportunities of contemporary life. The disparities lie in the difficulties Cubans have in acquiring these goods. This involves the gulf described above between those with the means to purchase goods in convertible pesos (CUC) on the black market and those continuing to rely on salaries or pensions in Cuban pesos (MN). VCRs were never available through the socialist distribution schemes that allowed Cubans to acquire other appliances. Unlike stereos and televisions available at high prices in dollar shops, VCRs were never officially for sale in Cuban retail outlets. In 2008, the same legislation that allowed Cubans to buy cell phone contracts permitted the sale of DVD players and home computers. Prior to this, only a very few Cubans could obtain home computers, and VCRs or DVDs that were "licensed" by the government for specific work-related purposes. Families with senior professionals at state enterprises might be permitted to buy a computer "with papers," or a senior media professional might have had a home VCR with papers. But before 2008, the principal method of acquiring such technologies was through the black market; home computers remained difficult to buy in this way due to size and cost, but VCR and DVD players became increasingly available. Their legalization in 2008 seems if anything to have bolstered the black market trade, as the prices for such goods in government stores remain higher than through informal networks.

VCRs, DVD players and computer parts have been brought into Cuba in a number of ways, and throughout the 1990s, seamen were commonly believed to be the major source of VCR players. The large numbers of professional workers sent overseas on "missions," working as doctors, engineers or consultants in developing countries, are permitted to send home large quantities of goods for personal use, and it is thought that many people use their quota to send home items to be resold by friends and family. A more personal, but still common, source for electronic goods is in the suitcases of Cuban emigrants or entrepreneurial tourists on return visits, although at various times customs prohibitions on such items have been enforced. In these and other ways, the very constraints that prevent many Cubans from media technologies have presented opportunities for profit, at least for those with access to international travel. This black market has not been consistently policed, as the Cuban government has chosen to ignore black market media technologies, focusing instead on policing the rare moments in which people use such media for explicitly counter-revolutionary protest. Other opportunities for profit lie in the rental of DVDs and other media, discussed in the context of mobile media circuits of consumption below.

Mobile Phones and Internet: A Path to Development?

As is so often the case with Cuba, the introduction of new information and communications technologies (ICTs) has differed from that of other nations in the Caribbean region, and has also been different from the methods adopted by other post-socialist nations such as Vietnam and China. For the most part, development in ICTs has been slow, in large part due to the trade embargo by the United States, which is the dominant player in telecommunications in the Americas, but also because of the internal economic, technological and political conditions of the Cuban state. Although television was successfully introduced in Cuba in the second half of the twentieth century, telephone service was less developed. Before 1959, Cuba had the highest telephone density in Latin America, but 73% of telephones were in Havana (Hoffmann 2004:189). Telephone infrastructure has not been highly developed regionally, and consequently Cuba has had one of the lowest telephone growth rates in the Latin American region. Since the 1960s, new telephone accounts have been distributed according to need and merit, so although costs are very low, waiting lists for a telephone are long, and even urban professionals with good social networks can wait years for a telephone line. To overcome this shortage, some people are assigned "community telephones," which are in individual houses, but can be used by anybody on request with a small fee. Even people who do not have community telephones inevitably end up operating a small informal service as the emergency contact number for neighbors or relatives who don't have a phone.

Cuba faces significant difficulties in improving the landline system and in setting up cellular and Internet service because of the U.S. trade embargo. Other nations in the Caribbean link fiber optic cables to the United States, and although these cables pass within 12 miles of Havana, no connection to Cuba has yet been made; digital data from Cuba must be relayed instead through satellite links (Coté, 2005). Since the mid-1990s, Italian and Mexican companies have digitized phone service in Cuba, increasing the number of landline telephones by more than 100% since 1994 (Hoffmann 2004:194). In 2009, Venezuela was laying fiber optic cables to Cuba just a few kilometers from Santiago, and these cables were expected to increase Cuba's Internet capacity 3,000-fold in 2011 (Reuters February 10 2011). It will be interesting to see how Cuban policymakers manage this increased level of access, as to date the genuinely low capacity of the Cuban cell and Internet networks has been the main reason for the limited access of Cuban consumers to new media and ICTs. The Cuban state has been ambivalent about the benefits of supporting these technologies. For example, in the early years of mobile phones, the technology was dismissed by Fidel Castro as being inappropriate for Cuban leaders "as a matter of austerity" (Hoffmann 2002:195). Even as Raúl Castro announced the legalization of mobile phones and personal computers, Internet accounts remain restricted. It is clearly the understanding of Cuban policymakers that new media technologies offer new opportunities for political and social change. Different technologies can be dealt with in different ways, so although television is promoted by the state, newer media technologies are either politely ignored (video/DVD), minimally developed (cell service), or actively restricted (Internet).

One of the noted reforms introduced by Raúl Castro in April 2008 was legalizing mobile phone contracts for Cubans. In the first 10 days after the ban was lifted, 7,400 new cell phone contracts were issued (BBC News April 24 2008). In a population of 11 million, this may seem modest when compared to smaller Caribbean countries such as Jamaica or Trinidad and Tobago, in which there are more mobile phone subscriptions than people (ITU 2009). But given the costs of over US $100 to initiate a contract with the state supplier when the average monthly salary is US $15 to $20, it seems clear that the change in policy has been received with enthusiasm by Cuban consumers. Officials estimate the sale of 1.4 million phone contracts by 2013; certainly between 2008 and 2009 the role of mobile phones in the everyday lives of better-off Cubans had increased dramatically, and ITU figures suggest that subscriptions rose from 2.96 to 5.54 per 100 inhabitants. In Cuba the high cost means that the typical cell phone owner is middle-aged and uses the phone primarily to keep in touch with family members abroad or, for example, to generate business for taxi service. Calls are around US 25 cents per minute, and contracts require payments of more than 10 CUC every two months even if no calls are made; as a result mobile phones are rarely used for actual conversations. Rather, people use them to receive or send text messages or to receive calls that they do not answer, instead responding by calling back from a pay phone. These sorts of money-saving tactics are similar to those found by other researchers of cell phone culture in low-income communities, in which cell phones have come to play a central role in everyday life to a degree that is to date not seen in Cuba.

Cuba connected to the Internet in 1996, although there was development in the 1980s of a Soviet-linked and domestic computer network (Mesher et. al. 1992). Cuba manages access by separating e-mail from Internet access. Although e-mail has been supported in workplace and community environments, since 2003 the Internet has been either unavailable or available only under controlled circumstances. Despite this prohibition, Cubans with access to computers and disposable income found ways to access the Internet to varying extents. Coté (2005) reports sales on the black market of pirated access codes, but a more common approach was to have a friendly foreigner set up an Internet account and then allocate this contract to a Cuban household. In 2004 I had an authorized domestic Internet account that I actually used myself. My application for the account had to be authorized by the university hosting my stay in Cuba, but the process was relatively straightforward. Although many workplaces have Internet access, connections are slow and individual workers have limited use. Unauthorized use to access illegal material such as pornography is policed and culprits are punished with long-term suspension from the Internet, or outright dismissal from their position. While Raúl Castro's reforms have allowed Cubans to start using the high-priced Internet cafés previously reserved for foreign tourists, several of my friends and informants were hesitant to make much use of such spaces. In addition to finding the registration of their ID card numbers intimidating, they worried that regularly spending the amounts required would publicly identify them as having a suspicious amount of money, making them as vulnerable to thieves and gossips as to the government.

Hard Drives as Mobile Media

Over the years that I have been following media consumption patterns in Cuba, from 2003 to 2010, the variety of film and television programs available, and the speed with which they arrive to Santiago de Cuba, have notably increased. The latest evidence of the acceleration of the informal media flows that supplement formal broadcasting channels is the use of external hard drives as mobile media devices by technology-literate Cubans, particularly the young and educated. In media studies, the term "mobile media" has been used to refer to the practices surrounding portable devices that are networked and/or based on cellular service (Goggin 2008). A body of literature has emerged examining global developments in which mobile phones, previously regarded as merely communication devices, are media devices as well, for viewing films, playing games and accessing the Internet. Anthropologists have been engaged in such research, not least because cell-phone technology has been heavily adopted among low-income communities, well beyond the Anglo-American strongholds typically featured in mainstream media scholarship. Mobile media have been shown to be especially appealing for consumers in places where the older infrastructures of broadcasting and telephone service are not easily accessed or developed; furthermore, many plans for mobile phones involve only small outlays of cash at regular intervals, making payment more manageable in the context of poverty or unpredictable income (Horst & Miller 2005; Slater & Kwami 2005; Pertierra et. al. 2002).

But in Cuba, where cell phones are used more rarely, a different kind of mobile media, the external hard drive, is having an important impact upon everyday media consumption. The technologically knowledgeable, rather than relying on an infrastructure to upload or download media content, use external hard drives connected to devices via USB or other ports to copy and move large amounts of media content between computers, for later viewing on media players or burned in CD or DVD format. It is the non-networked quality of portable hard drives that makes them an ideal technology in Cuba– they do not require a constant connection to electricity and are increasingly affordable. They can operate independently of Internet and computer networks, which are dependent on Cubans abroad to send money home for drives on the black market or bring them to Cuba when visiting. The use of external hard drives as mobile media is limited to those with a home computer and the technology to use such devices. Nonetheless, the use of hard drives to copy and circulate media content is affecting the wider community by increasing the diversity of media content available on the black market, allowing the development of generalist and specialist media rental services and almost immediate access to international shows and series. To give a sense of media consumption practices that are commonplace for people with access to hard drives, I present below Milene and Noel – both identifying as white, under 30, with a college education and relatives abroad. During my discussions I was struck that they regarded their access to and consumption of literally hundreds of television programs and films as normal, despite living in a country in which almost none of the hardware that supports their consumption habits can be bought in official shops, and in which all formal media channels are controlled by a centralized government that is officially hostile to globalized consumer culture. Just how this may be so, and why it seems to work, is addressed toward the end of this chapter.

Milene

Milene is a 20 year-old university student. She has her own laptop computer, which a relative bought for her. She has two external hard drives with capacities of 500MB and 250MB. Her smaller drive was bought overseas by relatives and given to her. The bigger drive was bought by other relatives in Spain and sent to Cuba via mutual friends. She has had the 500MB drive for five months, and the other for more than a year. Because Milene uses a computer for her studies, her family abroad send computer-related gifts to her rather than items such as clothes. But her computer and hard drives, she admits, are used for her leisure time as much as for her studies; since there's "nothing to do" in Santiago, she spends all her time at home. Milene describes her film and television viewing habits as a "vice," and she will often stay up until three a.m. to finish a television series, but she says she is far from abnormal in the number of shows she collects and watches, and that "70% of people her age do the same thing," at least among her circle of family and friends.

As we start to look at the contents, Milene says that she "copies everything," *("yo bajo de todo")* including series, films, soap operas, music, and Japanese *anime,* of which she is a fan. Although she doesn't know the person who downloads the material she gets, almost all of her hard drive contents come from one friend, who gets it from another friend. On the day of our conversation she remarked that the contents now were quite "old," by which she meant that she hadn't updated it for more than two weeks. Milene had 71 films stored, which was normal or perhaps on the low side for her, as she tends to delete films once she has watched them, and only keeps those that she thinks her sister might enjoy or that she regards as "classics," such as "Lord of the Rings" or "Silence of the Lambs." She rarely stores an entire series, and tends to copy them in installments, but Milene had 123 episodes of various television shows from the United States including "Battlestar Galactica," "Grey's Anatomy," "The Mentalist," and "One Tree Hill." Telenovelas she regards as a separate category, and although she does not watch them very attentively, Milene did have episodes from six different telenovelas stored on her hard drive (enough to fill between six and eight CDs). Milene tends not to store entire telenovela series, but they are so prevalent on the hard drives from which she copies – especially those from the Dominican Republic, Venezuela and Mexico – that she will watch them with her mother or friends. Many of her friends copy telenovela series even though they are broadcast on Cuban television, because it is "the fashion" to watch the broadcast to the end and find out what is going to happen before the national series has concluded.

In Milene's opinion, television series are most in demand among Cuban consumers, followed closely by music videos, with young people copying *reggaeton* music videos or audio files, which are easy to store in the hundreds as they take up less disc space. Milene has around 100 songs stored on her hard drive, which she describes as "mostly old." She is even less interested in other genres of television content that are found in the "packets" of audiovisual material that circulate in the city, listing reality shows, talk shows, the Grammy Awards, beauty pageants and "shows from Miami" as among the items that she does not burn, although many of her friends do. Instead she dedicates more than half of her hard drive space to the *anime* series that she loves, and on the day of our conversation Milene had 12 entire *anime* series, each containing approximately 50 episodes.

Because Milene knows many people in the circles of students and IT professionals who download small items or get free copies of films and television shows that are destined for rental businesses, she never pays for media content. In turn, she frequently copies films or television series for friends or family members to watch, either on computers or DVD players. Through her university friends, she has come into contact with people running successful rental businesses, including one acquaintance whom she describes as having a "a bookshelf full of more than 100 hard drives full of shows, and he rents them out." Another rental business specialized in copying old television shows from VHS to DVD, and this collection focused on Brazilian telenovelas and early U.S. hit shows that were popular among Cubans in the 1990s.

Noel

Noel is 25 years old and recently completed his engineering degree and now works for a government ministry. As his father works abroad and sends him remittances, Noel has had a computer at home for six or seven years, one of the first in the neighborhood. Just a few weeks before our interview in 2009, he had been sent a new external hard drive with a 500GB capacity from an overseas relative. Previously he had a 60GB external hard drive, which he has now installed in his computer. Before he had the external hard drive, Noel would sometimes remove his computer hard drive and take it with him to copy large quantities of media. But he found this a bother, and until 2008 Noel would most typically take two or three USB drives with a total capacity of around 10GB and look for something specific that he wanted to copy, such as an episode of a television series that he had missed.

Since acquiring a high-capacity portable drive, Noel has become less discriminate in the media he copies, although he still dislikes leaving too much content on his hard drive and tends to organize his files and delete the films and television series he has already watched. In our conversation we likened this tendency to keeping his room neat and tidy. Noel particularly enjoys films, and at the time of our interview he had copies of all of the 2009 Oscar-nominated films on his hard drive. By talking to friends or checking the Internet, Noel finds the list of nominees, and he and his friends share news about which films are circulating on the latest packets of audiovisual media so they can watch them before the Oscars are awarded. When a new packet arrives, Noel's friends let him know; he and his friends circulate media among themselves and with others for free, but he does know people in his neighborhood who use rental businesses regularly. If a typical packet contains between 30 and 40 films, Noel will begin by copying them all from his friend, and then deleting those of no interest, ending up with between six and nine films in his estimation. Noel explains that the contents of packets are mostly geared to the most rentable media, and are full of action films or other genres that he dislikes.

Although packets sometimes arrive weekly, Noel can spend up to a month waiting for new media that is worth his while to copy from friends. During our interview, Noel had not updated his hard drive for more than three weeks, and the most recent packet was numbered "Packet 191/192." In addition to several Oscar-nominated films, this packet included the bootleg version of "Wolverine" that had been circulating online.[65] Television series also took up much of Noel's hard drive space, and he had selections from more than 15 U.S. television series, including "24," "Prison Break," "Grey's Anatomy" and "The Sopranos." Although "Grey's Anatomy" and "The Sopranos" were being broadcast on Cuban television at the time, Noel had been watching the newer episodes to get ahead of the weekly broadcast. Like Milene, Noel listed a number of genres in the packets in which he was uninterested, and telenovelas, talk shows, reality shows, music compilations and wrestling were among the shows that some of his neighbors and friends enjoyed but that he disregarded.

The media rental businesses for which these packets are produced are not an entirely new phenomenon of the Cuban informal market. In the early 2000s, when video rental businesses were prospering in Santiago de Cuba, cassettes of films and occasionally older television series would circulate among business owners (Pertierra 2008). They originated in Havana, said to have been smuggled in from Mexico or videotaped from illegal satellite connections. This system was effective; it could take as little as three weeks to receive a popular film on videocassette in

---

[65] Media coverage internationally discussed the bootleg version of "Wolverine" being shown around April 2009, and Noel had copied this packet in July of the same year. This actually constitutes a fairly slow arrival in comparison to some of the other content referred to in this chapter.

Santiago de Cuba after cinematic release abroad. But new stock was not quickly replenished, and a typical video rental business would hold a catalogue of perhaps 40 titles at a given time because they needed to reuse videocassettes. In comparison, a hard drive with a capacity of 250MB, which in 2009 was no longer considered high capacity in Cuba, can store more than 200 television episodes or films, allowing illegal rental businesses to have a much wider range of stock. Furthermore, the ability to store films and other media on external drives makes downloading films, given Cuba's limited Internet network, more possible. Although I have not interviewed people engaged in such activities, a number of informants told me that IT administrators for large state operations with Internet accounts such as hotels or large workplaces will consolidate individual (that is, small) worker Internet quotas to download media content using file-sharing networks. Before downloading programs, software is downloaded that accommodates slow connections and downloads files in small parts over hours or days. Not all downloading takes place illegally; many of the most active in Santiago de Cuba are students whose have high-quota Internet access. IT students in other regions of Cuba have established websites on the Cuban intranet with files of films and television shows for download by fellow students.

The speed with which packets arrive in Santiago is frankly astonishing, and Noel only slightly exaggerates when he says, "If they show 'Prison Break' in the United States on a Wednesday, by Thursday it is here." In 2009, I watched television in Mexico and Miami for two weeks before arriving in Santiago de Cuba, and during my first week in Cuba, episodes of "Grey's Anatomy" broadcast in Mexico two weeks prior were already on Noel's hard drive. That same week, I talked to one of Noel's neighbors about a comedy show "Esta Noche Tonight," which broadcasts on the Miami channel Mega TV, and he had already seen one of the episodes in his packet that I watched 10 days earlier in Miami. Although the contrasts typically drawn between life in Cuba and life in Miami have never accurately portrayed the ongoing connections across the Florida Straits, the mobility of television programs in 2009 demonstrates the connections in almost real-time that increasingly characterize the consumption practices of urban Cubans, even if these are not representative of all sectors of the population.

As few Cubans have privileged Internet access, or even access to computers, in recent years there have emerged three circles of media user. In the inner circle are those who directly download programs from the Internet, which is largely undertaken for profit, but the contents are sufficiently low in value to be circulated for free among their friends. These friends also have access to portable hard drives, computers or viewers connected to a DVD player. Both Milene and Noel would be on the outer fringes of this inner circle. The second circle of media users are those with a DVD player at home, who rent content on discs for which they pay by the program, or they may rent a hard drive, for which they pay by the gigabyte. A third circle of media users are the majority of the Cuban population who do not have a DVD player at home and therefore are excluded from everyday non-broadcast media.

Such people are not necessarily excluded from the media culture, as visiting friends or relatives with DVD players is common, and many of the television series or films that circulate in packets are seen on Cuban television a few weeks or months later. Nevertheless, the policies of the Cuban government in limiting individual ownership or use of media and communications technologies have ironically created significant inequities in the Cuban population; it is the strong hierarchy emerging from very limited access to the Internet and computing technologies that allows a thriving trade in the rental of media content, the same media content that many people are copying and circulating for free.

Both Milene and Noel acknowledge that their computers and hard drives were invaluable gifts from close relatives abroad, and smaller peripherals have currency in the networks of sales and gifts through which so many consumer goods arrive in Cuba. Noel has a Spanish friend who regularly visits Cuba, and each visit he gives Noel a newer, larger USB device. Noel's Spanish friend will then take back the USB he had given Noel on his prior visit, and re-gift that smaller USB drive to another friend in town. In contrast to larger items such as hard drives, Noel describes USB drives as "cheap": they are easy to give away, lend or lose without much regret. Digital cameras, cables, adaptors, rechargeable batteries and recordable DVDs are also circulated among Cubans according to their needs and means. This is just one of the ways in which Cubans are perhaps more conscious than most media consumers of the "double articulation" of media technologies, as they are constantly aware of the material commodities required to support their continued engagement with the flow of media content that arrives speedily from "outside" (*afuera*).

New Media Policy in Cuba: Managing Resources versus Controlling Communication

Political scientist Bert Hoffmann argues that the development of the Internet in Cuba must be presented to state officials as something that is possible to control for political purposes. He suggests some development benefits have come from prioritizing Internet access by social/state institutions, which he describes as an "exclusive strategy" (2004: 205-215). In general, Hoffmann claims, the Cuban government "seeks to actively promote the 'Informatization of Society,' while emphasizing control and restricting individual Internet use." This negotiation between cultural producers, media users and state officials is publicly characterized by tolerance, but occasional examples are made of media that "crosses the line," for which producers are heavily sanctioned.[66] We can see similar dynamics in

---

[66] This typical management pattern of Cuban cultural production and information communication, and the limits that have been tested since the economic and political transformations of the 1990s, has been observed by several scholars. For example, DJs at Radio Taino, originally intended for tourists but actually popular with Cubans, pushed the limits of how much foreign music could be played and were censored (Hernandez Reguant 2002). At the same time, rap musicians, originally seen as subversive by imitating American forms, have been incorporated into state arts institutions (Baker 2005, Fernandes 2003).

debates between bloggers and state officials, in which the former test limits through exploring any new political or technological avenues, while state officials seem to operate with the discretion to allow some things while restricting others.

Since 2008, the focus of international reporting on Cuban new media policies has shifted from concerns about access to the Internet to include the active Cuban online production sector, chiefly evidenced in blogs. Obviously, there are significant obstacles to production for most of the population: first, in having access at all; second in having sufficient time at a computer and sufficient bandwidth to produce media; and third, in having the skills for website or blog production. A small group of educated youths– mostly computer science graduates and/or people with literary/artistic training—are using the Internet as an alternative space for debate and communication. A number of these blogs chronicle the experiences of everyday life in Havana, chiefly voicing the perspectives of young and highly educated Cubans who have an awareness of world as well as local events. As such, the emerging Cuban blogosphere is overtly "political" in ways that everyday conversations and mainstream media in Cuba is not, as a new generation of educated and skilled young citizens, mostly based in Havana, communicate perspectives that differ both from the much more visible blogging of Cuban emigrants and from the official websites of the Cuban state. The best known of these so-called *cibernauticos* (cybernauts) is Yoani Sanchez, whose *Generación Y* blog as received attention from international press and attracts hundreds of thousands of hits per week. Sanchez writes very critically about the Cuban government, and has written about intimidation from state officials. The Cuban government has not officially censored Sanchez, but her blog is unavailable when people try to access it within Cuba, and she was not granted a Cuban exit visa to travel to Spain in May 2008 in order to receive the prestigious Ortega y Gasset prize, awarded by the *El País* newspaper, for her digital journalism.

The *Generación Y* blog is a great case study of the problem the Cuban state faces in managing new media and information technologies as it navigates a path between restriction (to manage distribution of resources or to maintain state authority) and tolerance (because total control is impossible, and to demonstrate tolerance in order to justify sanctions.)

Why do new media seem to present such social and political problems for legislators, producers and consumers that were not features of old media? Old mass media and communications systems created common experiences of time and space; this has been an often observed characteristic of television, and it has proved as useful to socialist states as to liberal democracies in constructing national communities that share common consumption practices, engage in shared debates, and produce common understandings of time and space. In contrast, most research on new information technologies focuses on their capacity to "minimise previously existing barriers of time and space, including national boundaries" (Hoffmann 2004). Within democracies, information and communication are seen as crucial to the development of a public sphere, however, the introduction of such technologies is shaped by political and economic contexts and can include restrictions or unequal access as a result of political actions as well as an inevitable effect of market capitalism (Dunn 1995). Tension exists between the national interests of political organizations and governments and the transnational character and power of new communications technologies (Hoffmann 2004). Indeed, even older electronic media such as television – a medium that is often thought of as national, and nationalist – are heavily shaped by transnational commercial forces. The increasing delivery of television content through new media platforms, the commercialization of many broadcast industries and the growth of multinational television industries have created a "post-broadcast era" in which the national interests of a government determine less about broadcast television than before (Turner and Tay 2009). Similarly, news media in the small nations of Latin America and the Caribbean have long been regarded as heavily dependent upon transnational news networks for information about each other, and often about themselves (Klak 1994). Therefore, although this chapter has shown genuine differences between older and newer media forms, there is also evidence that the increasingly transnational character of media commerce has affected the politics of all media use.

Further complicating the popular Western image of socialist media as all about censorship is the socialist love of science and technological achievement. Since the 1980s

Cuba has been at the forefront of technological development in some areas, including biotechnology (Reid-Henry 2007), and it has also pursued with less success the goal of making Cuban universities hubs of information technology for Latin America and the rest of the developing world (Mesher et al. 1992). This history of championing science and technology as the means through which economic and social inequalities can be overcome contributes to the government's ambivalent attitude to the introduction of new media and technologies into everyday life. Although information can be problematic, it can also be revolutionary; consequently technology may be championed in Cuba even while the state attempts to control how, why and by whom particular information, communications and technologies can be deployed. As each new medium or technology is widely adopted not only in affluent societies, but also in more modest developing nations, Cuban policymakers regard each innovation on a case-by-case basis to evaluate how best to juggle competing interests and concerns. In turn, media users and cultural producers take advantage of oversights in government attention and changes in policy to maximize their use of media, at times pushing the limits of control, which in turns prompts further shifts in policy. In so doing, they follow in the footsteps of writers, artists, journalists, religious leaders and others who have combined strategies of collaboration with the leveraging of transnational resources to operate and create in contemporary civil society (Hernandez-Reguant 2009; Hearn 2008).

transnation media

The media landscape of Cuba is characterized by a deep connection to transnational circuits of media consumption despite the official isolation of the Cuban media industries and the technological isolation that limits the everyday connectivity of most Cubans to new media and information technologies. Transnational circuits of media and communication are not new– indeed, Cuba's isolation from the United States is often expressed or reinforced by the messages in letters, phone calls, songs and videos that have long traveled back and forth in what Lisa Maya Knauer terms "audiovisual remittances" (Knauer 2009; see also Settle 2008 on letters). This deep connection to transnational circuits of media consumption is like the other forms of consumption experienced by Cubans as problematic, and even political, but not in the way that most international journalism has framed analyses of the politics of media consumption in Cuba. Global press attention focuses on the limitations placed on Cubans in their access to media by the effects of U.S. hostility toward Cuban technological development, and also on the Cuban government's ambivalence toward the social and political consequences of rapid new media access. But such press attention gives the impression that Cubans are effectively isolated from the popular culture shared in the rest of the Americas by way of transnational and commercial mass media. This impression is far from the truth; although Cubans complain about the dullness of nationally produced television programs, or about the prohibitive prices of media technologies, at the same time they engage daily in the consumption of transnational media that is either legal and state-supported (as in the case of television), or largely informal but clearly tolerated (as in the case of the circulation of media through DVDs and hard drives).

For the most part, Cubans seek to supplement their television viewing with other media, not to access entertainment that is prohibited via state broadcasting, but rather to increase the hours of leisure time spent watching films and television, to "time-shift" their viewing outside the broadcast schedule, to seek out special titles or genres that are not prohibited and to share media as a social practice by which relationships are maintained and, in some cases, profits are gained. Although there is undoubtedly deeply illegal activity that does take place within the circuits of media sharing I have described above – anti-Castro satire, political documentaries and pornography do of course travel along these routes– for the most part media sharing and consumption is not problematic because of the content enjoyed. This is not only true of television, but also of the copied and downloaded media that Milene and Noel were sharing with friends; each separately clearly stated that they engaged in these activities openly and that the authorities were aware of the circulation of packets and did not prohibit downloading by individual students and IT professionals. As Milene said, such downloading was permitted *para que los muchachos se tranquilizen* [so the young people relax], while Noel insisted that *a nadie le importa todo esto* [nobody cares about this]. In a related conversation with my informant Pablo, who is knowledgeable about telecommunications, we discussed a similar question in relation to mobile phones, which in 2009 had recently become legal for personal use but remained both expensive and unreliable. I asked Pablo whether he believed that mobile phone use in Cuba had been intentionally limited by the government as a form of censorship to stifle potential political dissent or prevent antirevolutionary organizing. His response was representative of what a number of people, with a range of attitudes to the current state of affairs in Cuba, told me:

> Here in Cuba, nobody is talking about stuff like that – that's the sort of thing people always talk about outside Cuba. The problem in Cuba – apart from the situation with the North Americans which has always been tense – but the thing in Cuba is, I don't think the Cuban government will change because people talk more or less than before because they have cellphones. I don't think so, no. And the Cuban government doesn't think so either, but it really is a big investment [to build a cellphone network]. An expensive investment. We are a poor country, with a lot of social services commitments, which have to be maintained. That isn't a lie, it is real – it is a reality. And that development of the network is happening, but little by little.

My research has suggested that most Cubans are troubled not by censorship or political agitation, but by the politics and economics of *access* to media technologies such as DVD players and personal computers. People express resentments, vulnerabilities and concerns about the widening gap between those who have access to the growing range of media technologies and those who do not, as what looks like a resurgent middle class of Cubans, who are technologically literate, highly educated and with disposable income, devote more of their leisure time to media consumption that takes place behind closed doors. Poorer Cubans, through government initiatives that introduced audiovisual technologies to schools and workplaces, are often enjoying identical television content, for example, but to a lesser extent and in a different domestic context.

Residents with well-equipped households are increasingly concerned about theft and home security, and their poorer neighbors are inevitably aware of the material signs of upward mobility that cannot be entirely hidden. Therefore the economic prosperity required to buy expensive media technologies and the retreat into privacy that new media consumption practices enable, can be sources of suspicion. But at the same time, the appeal of maximizing the potential to enjoy and schedule leisure and entertainment within the home is consistent with the centrality of the domestic sphere to respectable family life.

Of course, it is in precisely this way that televisions, DVD players, hard drives and other media technologies can be seen to have a deeply political role within the framework of contemporary socialism. To draw from wider media research, Cuban media consumers might be thought of as being either duped into allowing continuation of the Cuban regime or, alternatively, engaging in small-scale acts of resistance by choosing to consume "apolitical" popular culture within a deeply politicized society.[67] I agree with

---

[67] A vast body of media research has analyzed the autonomy (or lack thereof) of consumers to accept or resist dominant interpretations of media that are encouraged by commercial and state interests; just a few

anthropologist Amelia Weinreb's (2007) analysis that the
Special Period resulted in a retreat of the Cuban middle
classes from civic activity as an alternative to explicit
resistance, but I also believe that we should take seriously
how and why this retreat, which includes the expanded
consumption of media at home, is understood by most
Cubans as being entirely appropriate in the context of
Cuban socialism. Although escaping politics to watch
television may be an act with political consequences, that it
is not primarily understood as a political act by the person
watching television is also important. To return to one of
the points beginning this chapter, recognizing the
similarities of Cuban media consumption to that of other
countries in the Latin American region is useful in
delineating the differences, and the fact that most Cubans
seek media content similar to their Hispanic Caribbean
neighbors, with the same purpose of leisure and
entertainment, is not negated by the economic and political
framework that requires them to take very different paths to
establish the material requirements of such consumption.

---

of the best known contributors to this research include Jean Baudrillard
(1981), Stuart Hall (1991), and Ien Ang (1985). Various examples of
specifically ethnographic contributions to debates surrounding the
power structures and cultural politics of media production and
consumption can be found in Askew & Wilk's *The Anthropology of
Media: A Reader,* in which Parts 2 to 5 focus on the implications of
representation (of the self and of others), on the capacity of audiences
to appropriate locally and internationally produced media, and on the
impact of such power structures as colonialism and nationalism on
media practices (Askew & Wilk 2002).

Conclusion

A Politics of Cuban Consumption

When people find out that I have spent time in Cuba, they usually ask me two questions. First, are Cubans happy with Fidel Castro and, more recently, with his brother Raúl? Second, what will happen in Cuba when socialism ends? Cubans living abroad are also asked these questions and, for them more than me, dread such questions; impossible to answer, uncomfortable to address, tedious to repeat and distasteful to raise in polite company. Most people who ask these questions do not intend to create discomfort, and I do not assume that my own reasons for hesitating to answer them are the same as those of my Cuban friends, colleagues, relatives and informants. But as someone who has thought extensively about those dreaded questions, and whose understanding of what those questions even mean has changed during the course of research, I would like to begin by discussing why they are so natural to "outsiders" but are so uncomfortable to "insiders."

The questions, and the frequency with which they are asked, suggest several assumptions about Cuba. One assumption is that Fidel Castro was omnipresent, until he wasn't, and that this transition must be spectacular news.

Another assumption is that Cuban socialism is a coherent, cohesive, monolithic structure of state institutions and imposed-upon citizens. A third assumption is that Cubans have a deep knowledge and understanding of their political situation, which they can and want to articulate in terms that would make sense to non-Cubans. Across all of these assumptions is the idea that what makes Cuba interesting is its unique and enduring role within the geopolitics of the post-Cold War Americas. But what makes Cuba interesting internationally is not what Cubans themselves are most interested in thinking or talking about when they assess their quality of life, consider their memories of the past or articulate their hopes for the future. Through the practices and experiences of people in this study, I have tried to show that these assessments take place not in the sphere of political debate, but rather in the sphere of consumption and the struggles consumption has presented since the 1990s. For people interested in how Cubans understand and assess their social, economic and political position, using the questions of outsiders cited above is not the best starting point: it presupposes a political debate that is uninteresting, insufficient or uncomfortable for a number of reasons that are briefly mentioned before moving on to explain how and why a study of consumption might ultimately be a better way to understand Cuba.

Most Cubans do not easily proffer candid opinions about their government. Obviously this is due in no small part to the authoritarian nature of Cuban governance, but individual reasons for avoiding political discussions are varied and complex and should not be reduced to a simple fear of retribution. Privately, some Cubans are strongly critical of their government or specific policies or indeed Fidel or Raúl Castro. More frequently, people have quite openly expressed disappointment or bitterness about how the revolution has failed to provide the envisioned future that they and their comrades were working toward. Many are cynical about the objectivity of news and current affairs broadcasts, and feel that only some kinds of information about national affairs are ever released to the public. But the vast majority of Cubans I have known – including those who are ambivalent or skeptical about the viability of socialism in the twenty-first century – also refute vigorously the depictions of Cuba that they see from U.S. émigré political groups or from sectors of the U.S. media. Cubans typically acknowledge that the U.S. trade embargo has created an immensely difficult economic situation for the Cuban government, and almost all accept in principle state-controlled distribution of health care, education, food and other basic services to all citizens. But most people also have a long list of examples showing that the rhetoric of the Cuban government has in reality fallen short, and that many schemes are either poorly administered or fail to acknowledge the ways in which Cubans feel they are being denied resources and opportunities. Such nuanced perspectives are difficult to express on a topic as fraught as Cuba, in which many discussants are keen to attack, critique or amend information to support larger ideological or political debates.

Cubans (and even scholars of Cuba!) are often called upon by people to represent and explain a complex political reality, and ultimately to judge it in a way rarely expected when discussing other nations. In practice, most individual attitudes are too complicated to neatly package in a way that would satisfy the curiosity of most questioners, and the prevailing sense among Cubans that their own society is exceptionally complex discourages all but the most articulate and enthusiastic public speakers from attempting an analysis of Cuban politics that is honest, polite and comprehensible to outsiders.

Furthermore, many Cubans – and not only the young who grew up after the glories of the Soviet era – claim to be entirely uninterested in politics, and express no more opinion about the subject than a general cynicism about the ongoing discourse that pervades both Cuban and U.S. commentaries. For the sizeable group in this category, this response should be taken seriously and not dismissed as a cover for unspoken fear or hatred of Cuban socialism per se.

This book has shown how state policies have affected how households are constituted, how family relationships affect the opportunities available to Cubans and how the material contents of a house can be the result of political engagement. With the changing landscape of media consumption, I have shown that for some Cubans it is increasingly possible to engage in leisure activities that bypass the national media infrastructure central to the communication of state policy and that access to such leisure practices is limited to sectors of the population that are highly integrated into the Cuban political structure. These practices, each related to mass consumption, are all in some sense "political," but that is not their intention. As discussed in the first chapter of this book, however, it is in discussing these consumption practices – frequent discussions with candor and enthusiasm – that most people confront and negotiate the political and moral realities of contemporary Cuba.

Studying Cuban Consumption, or Scholarly Consumption of Cuba?

In the first volume of the new *Journal of Consumer Culture,* Daniel Miller in 2001 presented a critique of moralizing stances that dominated research on modern consumption, arguing that such stances effectively reduced research to a performance of the scholar's own political position. Too many theorists of consumption, he argued, equated mass consumption with superficial emptiness and materialism, which said much more about the dangers of over-consumption in specific wealthy communities (that is, those of the researchers) than it did about anything else. Drawing from the work of sociologist E.P. Thompson on the English working class, Miller describes such approaches as a "Poverty of Morality," in which simplistic assumptions about capitalism and/or Americanization has led researchers to studies that confirmed their own moral stances. What was needed instead, argued Miller, was more grounded observation of how consumption takes place, and of how such consumption is understood by diverse groups of people in their everyday lives. Drawing from fieldwork in the United Kingdom, Trinidad and India, Miller suggested that, far from feeling guilty, overwhelmed or alienated by the increasing abundance of contemporary consumer goods, it was often impoverished people for whom material goods were the most delightful, important or worthy of labor and sacrifice (Miller 2001:232). In such contexts, anthropologists and other scholars should consider that consumer culture brings enjoyment and enhances sociability as often as not. At the very least, the enthusiasm with which many people around the world seek greater opportunities for consumption should be regarded as a serious topic worthy of empathetic rather than moralistic study.

Since Miller's critique was published, consumption studies have proliferated, and there is good ethnographic research that documents the embrace of consumption in a range of localities, not least in Latin America and the Caribbean. In 2010 the same *Journal of Consumer Culture* in which Miller's "Poverty of Morality" piece was published a decade earlier returned to the question of moral stances in consumption studies with a roundtable of senior scholars in the field (Juliet Schor, Don Slater, Sharon Zukin and Viviana A. Zelizer). All argued the value of studying ethnographically and empathetically *how* and *why* people so often locate morality in the sphere of consumption. Some maintained "It is possible to make critical arguments about the mix of goods and services which are not rooted in the personal preferences of researchers" (Schor et.al. 2010:277), and there was also a warning against the tendency to "constitute the entire study of consumption around the agenda of specifically northern moral panics, guilt complexes, class tastes and intellectual traditions" (Schor et.al. 2010:281). Even if there is a desire to judge acts of consumption as unethical, immoral or undesirable, what sociologist Viviana A. Zelizer describes as "moral agnosticism" can only be abandoned *after* empirical research into the actual consumption practices (Schor et.al. 2010:290-291).

Calls for research that is more empathetic and less moralistic are always welcome to an anthropologist, and in keeping with the trend of the "ethnographic (re)turn" across the humanities and social sciences, anthropological approaches have been essential to the field of consumption studies. Calls for such research are particularly welcome for Cuban studies, which as a whole has been similarly dominated by research in which the critical and moral stances of the author take precedence over what Cubans may actually be doing in everyday life.

I suggest that in scholarship as much as in other contexts, "Cuba" has predominantly come to be a symbol more than an actual place in which people live and interact. For some, Cuba is a symbol of oppression, tyranny and poverty, and for some Cuban-Americans it is the symbol of a lost past, of nostalgia and displacement. For many of the increasing number of tourists, Cuba is a symbol of superb cultural expression, of rich artistic and musical forms combining high art, popular culture and folk traditions. For others, Cuba symbolizes the possibility of new embodied experiences, whether through the sexual liberation imagined in romantic encounters or through spiritual transcendence sought by adherents of Afro-Cuban religious sects. For a number of progressive activists and intellectuals, Cuba remains a symbol of hope or inspiration, and Cuba has long played this role in European and Latin American leftist movements. Cuban intellectual Roberto Fernández Retamar has described this as the "enormity" of Cuba: "This is what makes Cuba different: its abnormality, its enormity (which by no means contradicts the smallness of its territory, population, and resources)" (Fernández Retamar & Beverley 1996: 188). To provide just one example, Fernández Retamar cites the Brazilian scholar Darcy Ribeiro, who described Cuba's mere existence as an "unbearable" proof that Latin Americans could achieve a "supreme utopia" (Fernández Retamar & Beverley 1996:189).

But no imagined or symbolic Cuba – no matter how enormous, exceptional or unbearable – should be confused with the 11 million people currently living in a range of circumstances on an actual island in the Caribbean. I am not arguing that Cuba should never be studied for its symbolic or semiotic significance, nor that scholarship on Cuba should shy away entirely from taking critical and moral stances. However, such approaches should not be the only way in which Cuba is represented in international scholarship, and the sort of empathetic empirical research of anthropologists across the world is insufficiently represented in current Cuban research. As demonstrated throughout this book, Cubans' attitudes towards consumption do not fit into simple categories such as "socialist" or "anti-socialist." To attempt to fit Cuban consumption within a moral or political framework of "good" versus "bad," or "socialist" versus "capitalist" or "empowered" versus "duped" would not be a study of

Cuban consumption, but rather the consuming of Cuba as a symbol for the purposes of wider external debates.

Therefore, the politics of Cuban consumption of interest are found first in the effects of the Cuban political and economic situation on the experiences and practices of Cuban people before turning to theorization about the political consequences of contemporary Cuba for either the Cuban people or the world. My conclusion is that in everyday life in Cuba, politics is most explicitly and most powerfully played out through the practices and discussions that relate to the acquisition of consumer goods. It is in the practices that Cubans undertake to buy, keep, win, fix or steal commodities that they most express their dissatisfaction, react to government policies, measure their happiness, care for their families and work toward their futures. It is in understanding the human practices and relations that surround and engage the material culture of mass consumption that the shifting positions and perspectives of the Cuban people are most clearly located. Cubans experience and evaluate their society primarily by the difficulties they experience in such activities as lining up for rations and buying expensive groceries in dollar stores. They measure self-worth in their ability to overcome such difficulties, by being flexible and sociable small-business owners and by piecing together domestic interiors that bring pleasure, comfort and respectability to their loved ones. The growing material inequity between citizens in contemporary Cuba, and the social differentiation that results, is being mapped primarily through the new leisure practices made possible by media and communications technologies in a society where cash incomes are only a partial indicator of economic status, and determinants of social class have been transformed first by socialism and subsequently by the Special Period. Consumption practices, and the interaction and discussion that they provoke, provide some of the most powerful and poignant experiences from which an understanding can develop of the difficulties with which Cubans and their government negotiate life and livelihood in the twenty-first century.

So perhaps a more effective way to reframe the questions at the beginning of this chapter is to ask how and where do Cubans confront their happiness or unhappiness with the current political and economic state of Cuba? As the politics and economics of Cuba change, what will be the measure by which Cubans consider their lives improved or otherwise? These are the questions that I, at least, would be much happier to attempt answering, although my Cuban friends, colleagues, relatives and informants, whose views on this subject I by no means represent, may feel differently. And my answer to both questions is: in the practices, experiences and struggles of mass consumption.

Perhaps more than other sphere of everyday life, future opportunities for consumption will dictate how quality of life is measured by Cubans, whether in the framework of socialism or not. It is also in consumption that the most unrest in the Cuban population is explicitly located. Particularly with and since the Special Period, the Cuban government has allowed and acknowledged the vocal frustration of its citizens on matters of consumption, not only as part of the greater arena of civil society, but also because of the history of mass consumption, socialist or not, that Cubans regard not only as desirable but as a right. It is by engaging in mass consumption that people in Cuba negotiate the complex transitions and cultural continuities that characterize daily life in places such as Santiago de Cuba. The desire for easily obtained and affordable consumer goods that the women and men featured in this book frequently expressed is not necessarily an expression of resistance to socialism, or of an embrace of the global consumer culture, but is rather the latest manifestation of a long history in which an important aspect of the Cuban idea of self lies in their consumer practices.

The End of the Special Period?

The post-Soviet era, which has also been described as "late socialism," has been experienced and understood as a specific historical epoch, or what Ariana Hernandez Reguant has called a "defining category of experience" (2009:1), and the intent of this book has been to capture and explain the prominence of consumption practices and consumer goods within this category of experience. The Special Period had a clear beginning, but its end has been less easy to identify; in some ways, the 1990s brought a specific harshness and shock that by the time of my fieldwork had worn off. In other ways, the key practices of struggle, invention and acquisition have remained at the center of daily life in an economic configuration that is no longer a period of "transition" but a now-familiar negotiation between individual Cubans and state institutions, which is regularly adjusted according to global market forces, internal and international political situations and to social and cultural changes within Cuba.

Looking to the future of Cuba–a subject that has consumed much scholarly, political and popular attention– it seems clear that the path will continue to be defined by the priority that Cuban citizens give to mass-produced commodities for their basic survival, as well for as leisure or pleasure. Given that this priority has been actively – if not always effectively – addressed within Cuban socialism, there is less reason at the time of writing than at the onset of the Special Period to assume that socialism will disappear anytime soon, even if market reforms of the kind announced by Raúl Castro in 2008 and 2010 transform some aspects of daily life in important ways.

Cuba's relationship with Venezuela should not be underestimated as a means for retaining socialism as the prevailing politico-economic doctrine. Venezuela has significantly boosted the Cuban economy, providing subsidized oil and accounting for over 68% of Cuba's trade with Latin America and for 25% of Cuba's international trade in 2008. In return for the goods that arrive from Venezuela, Cuba exports human resources in the way of doctors and other professionals (Erikson & Wander 2009:14-15). Other left-leaning countries in Latin America such as Bolivia, Ecuador, Nicaragua, and (until the 2009 coup) Honduras have also engaged in diplomatic, economic and political relations with Cuba, and Brazil under the presidency of Lula da Silva worked to reconnect Cuba politically with South American nations. China has noticeably increased political and economic relations with Cuba, and trade increased by over 500% between 2003 and 2008 (Erikson & Wander 2009:21). Cuba has been part of the broader Chinese push to build an export market in Latin America, invest in new sources of minerals and energy and build political alliances in international organizations to serve as counterweights to the United States and European Union (Hearn 2006; Dreyer 2006). Russia and Cuba are overcoming the difficulties and hostilities that were a consequence of the *perestroika* process, and high-level military visits between the two countries since 2008 have been noted with interest by the press and international affairs specialists.

Clearly, Cuban socialism is far from dead, although it has changed and adapted many times. The process of developing this project on Cuban consumption, from the earliest stages of my doctoral fieldwork until the completion of this manuscript, happened to map the final years of leadership of Fidel Castro and the takeover by his brother Raúl. The uncertainties and reforms being closely watched by the world press raise questions about whether this ethnography might serve as something more than a snapshot of an existence that is soon to disappear or a recycled version of the anthropologist as documenter of a "Disappearing World." In this Conclusion I have tried to show why I think that the most radical changes to Cuban society are unlikely to end the mundane practices of everyday life and orientation to material goods in which this ethnography is grounded. Without wanting to join the choruses that have assured us of the decline of Cuban socialism for almost 50 years, I suspect that a post-Castro Cuba will bring new permutations of the struggle for consumption that require understanding the social production of scarcity that has been so definitive of Cuba in moving from the twentieth into the twenty-first century.

Bibliography

Alén Rodriguez, O. 1991. "The Tumba Francesa Societies and their Music," in Manuel, P. (ed.) *Essays on Cuban Music: North American and Cuban Perspectives.* London: University Press of America, pp. 75-85.

Alexandre, L. 1992. "Television Martí: Electronic Invasion in the Post-Cold War," *Media Culture Society* 14:523-540.

Ang, I. 1985. *Watching Dallas: Soap Opera and the Melodramatic Imagination.* (Couling, C., trans.) London: Methuen.

Appadurai, A. 1996. *Modernity at Large: Cultural Dimensions of Globalization.* Minneapolis: University of Minnesota Press.

Askew, K. & Wilk, R. (eds). *The Anthropology of Media: A Reader.* London: Blackwell Publishers.

Baker, G. 2005. ¡Hip Hop Revolución! Nationalizing Rap in Cuba, *Ethnomusicology* Vol 49(3):368-402.

Barnard, A. & Spencer, J. (eds). 1996. *Encyclopedia of Social and Cultural Anthropology.* London and New York: Routledge.

Baudrillard, J. 1981. *For a Critique of the Political Economy of the Sign.* (Levin, C. trans.) St Louis: Telos Press.

Benjamin, M., Collins, J. & Scott, M. 1986. *No Free Lunch: Food and Revolution in Cuba Today.* New York: Grove Press.

Bentley, A. 1998. *Eating for Victory: Food Rationing and the Politics of Domesticity.* Champaign: University of Illinois Press.

Berdahl, D. 1999. *Where the World Ended: Re-unification and Identity in the German Borderland.* Berkeley: University of California Press.

Bettelheim, J. 1991. "Negotiations of Power in Carnaval Culture in Santiago de Cuba," *African Arts* Vol 24(2): 66-75; 91-2.

Bourdieu, P. 1984. *Distinction: A Social Critique of the Judgment of Taste* (Nice, R. trans.) New York and London: Routledge.

Buchli, V. 2000. *An Archaeology of Socialism.* Oxford: Berg.

Búriková, Z. 2003. "Christian" Shops: Morality and Commerce in the Slovak Village. *Anthropological Journal on European Cultures* Vol12:187-204.

_____. 2006. The Embarrassment of Co-Presence: Au Pairs and their Rooms. *Home Cultures* Vol 3(2): 99-122.

Burke, T. 1996. *Lifebuoy Men, Lux Women.* Durham: Duke University Press.

Butterworth, D. 1974. "Grass-Roots Political Organization in Cuba: A Case of the Committees for the Defense of the Revolution." In Cornelius, W.A. and Trueblood, F.M. (eds.) *Latin American Urban Research Volume 4: Anthropological Perspectives on Latin American Urbanization.* London: Sage Publications, pp 183-205.

Caldwell, M. 2004. *Not by Bread Alone: Social Support in the New Russia.* Berkeley: University of California Press.

Carlson, D. 2009. "Sugar, the Sweetener; Coffee, the Tonic; and Tobacco, the Narcotic of Half the World: Santiago de Cuba, Guantanamo, and the Windward Passage in the 19th Century."

Conference paper, International Congress of the Latin American Studies Association, Rio de Janeiro, June, 2009.

Castells, M. & Portes, A. 1989. "World Underneath: The Origins, Dynamics and Effects of the Informal Economy." Portes, A., Castells, M. & Benton, L.A (eds.) *The Informal Economy: Studies in Advanced and Less Developed Countries.* London: Johns Hopkins University Press, pp.11-40.

Castro Ruz, Fidel. 1990. Speech at the closing of the 16th Congress of the CTC, Karl Marx Theatre, 28 January 1990. [Discurso pronunciado por Fidel Castro Ruz, Presidente de la República de Cuba, en la Clausura del XVI Congreso de la CTC, celebrado en el Teatro "Carlos Marx", el 28 de enero de 1990, "Año 32 de la Revolución."] http://www.cuba.cu/gobierno/discursos/1990/esp/f280190e.html downloaded 17 March, 2006.

_____. 2006. Speech delivered by Fidel Castro Ruz, president of the Republic of Cuba, on the occasion of the 47th anniversary of his entry into the province of Pinar del Río at the ceremony held in celebration of the successful installation of electric power generators in this province. Pinar del Río, 17 January 2006, "Year of the Energy Revolution in Cuba." [Discurso pronunciado por Fidel Castro Ruz, Presidente de la República de Cuba, en ocasión del aniversario 47 de su entrada en Pinar del Río, en el acto por la culminación del montaje de los grupos electrógenos en esa provincia. Pinar del Río, 17 de enero de 2006.] http://www.cuba.cu/gobierno/discursos/2006/esp/f170106e.html downloaded 11 April, 2006.

Chant, S. with Craske, N. 2003. *Gender in Latin America.* London: Latin America Bureau.

Chávez, L. (ed.) 2005. *Capitalism, God, and a Good Cigar: Cuba Enters the Twenty-First Century.* Durham and London: Duke University Press.

Cornelius, W.A. 1974. "Introduction." In Cornelius, W.A. and Trueblood, F.M. (eds.) *Latin American Urban Research Volume 4: Anthropological Perspectives on Latin American Urbanization.* London: Sage Publications, pp 9-23.

Coté, J. 2005. "Cubans Log on Behind Castro's Back." In Chávez, L. (ed.) *Capitalism, God, and a Good Cigar: Cuba Enters the Twenty-First Century.* Durham and London: Duke University Press, pp. 160-76.

Cowan, R. S. 1983. *More Work for Mother: The Ironies of Household Technology from the Open Hearth to the Microwave.* New York: Basic Books.

De Certeau, M, Giard, L. & Mayol, P. 1998. *The Practice of Everyday Life: Living and Cooking.* Minneapolis: University of Minnesota Press.

De La Torre, M.A. 2003. *La Lucha for Cuba: Religion and Politics on the Streets of Miami.* Berkeley: University of California Press.

Drakulic, S. 1992. *How We Survived Communism and Even Laughed.* London: Hutchinson.

Dreyer, J.T. 2006. "From China With Love: P.R.C. Overtures in Latin America," *Brown Journal of World Affairs* Vol XII, Issue 2: 85-98.

Dunn, H.S. 1995. "Policy Issues in Communications Technology Use: Challenges and Options." In Dunn, H. S. (ed.) *Globalization, Communications and Caribbean Identity.* New York: Routledge.

Eckstein, S.E. 2003. *Back from the Future: Cuba under Castro*, 2nd ed. New York: Routledge.

Economist Intelligence Unit. 2004. *Country Report: Cuba.* London: Economist Intelligence Unit.

_____. 2006. *Country Report: Cuba.* London: Economist Intelligence Unit.

Enríquez, L. J. 1994. *The Question of Food Security in Cuban Socialism.* Berkeley: University of California International and Area Studies.

_____. 2003. "Economic Reform and Repeasantization in post-1990 Cuba," *Latin American Research Review* Vol. 38(1): 202 – 217.

Erikson, D.P. & Wander, P.J. "Cuba's Brave New World," *Fletcher's Forum of World Affairs* Vol 33(2):9-28.

Ferguson, J. 1999. *Expectations of Modernity: Myths and Meanings of Urban Life on the Zambian Copperbelt.* Berkeley: University of California Press.

Fernandes, S.J. 2003. "Island Paradise, Revolutionary Utopia or Hustler's Haven? Consumerism and Socialism in Contemporary Cuban Rap," *Journal of Latin American Cultural Studies* 12 (3):359 – 375.

Fernández, D. 2000. *Cuba and the Politics of Passion.* Austin: University of Texas Press.

Fernández, N. 1999. "Back to the Future: Women, Race and Tourism in Cuba". In Kempadoo, K. (ed.) *Sun, Sex and Gold: Tourism and Sex Work in the Caribbean.* Lanham, MD: Rowman & Littlefield.

Fernández Retamar, R. & Beverley, J. 1996. "The Enormity of Cuba," *boundary 2,* Vol 23 (3):165-190.

Font, M. and Larson, S. (eds.) *Cuba in Transition? Pathways to Renewal, Long-Term Development, and Global Reintegration.* New York: CUNY Graduate Center, pp. 143-158.

_____. 2008. *Cuba: Religion, Social Capital and Development.* Durham: Duke University Press.

Foster, R.J. 2002. *Materializing the Nation: Commodities, Consumption and Media in Papua New Guinea.* Bloomington: Indiana University Press.

Friedmann, J., Abers, R. & Autler, L. (eds). 1996. *Emergences: Women's Struggles for Livelihood in Latin America.* Los Angeles: UCLA Latin American Center Publications.

Gal, S. & Kligman, G. 2000. *The Politics of Gender after Socialism: A Comparative-Historical Essay.* Princeton: Princeton University Press.

Galeano, E. 1997 [1973]. *Open Veins of Latin America: Five Centuries of the Pillage of a Continent.* (C. Belfrage, trans.) New York: Monthly Review Press.

Goggin, G. 2008. "The Models and Politics of Mobile Media," *The Fibreculture Journal* Vol 12. http://twelve.fibreculturejournal.org/fcj-082-the-models-and-politics-of-mobile-media/

González de la Rocha, M. 1995. "The Urban Family and Poverty in Latin America," *Latin American Perspectives,* Vol. 22 (2): 12-31.

Goody, J. 1982. *Cooking, Cuisine and Class: A Study in Comparative Sociology.* Cambridge: Cambridge University Press.

Gott, R. 2004. *Cuba: A New History.* New Haven and London: Yale University Press.

Gray, A. 1992. *Video Playtime: The Gendering of a Leisure Technology.* London: Routledge.

Gronow, J. 2003. *Caviar with Champagne: Common Luxury and the Ideals of the Good Life in Stalin's Russia.* Oxford: Berg.

Gudeman, S. & Rivera, A. 1990. *Conversations in Colombia: The Domestic Economy in Life and Text.* Cambridge: Cambridge University Press.

Hall, S. 1992. "Encoding/Decoding." In Hall, S. et al (eds.) *Culture, Media, Language: Working Papers in Cultural Studies, 1972-79.* London: Routledge.

Hart, K. 1973. "Informal Income Opportunities and Urban Employment in Ghana," *Journal of Modern African Studies* Vol 11(1):61-89.

_____. 2000. "Kinship, Contract, and Trust: The Economic Organization of Migrants in an African City Slum." In Gambetta, D. (ed.) *Trust: Making and Breaking Cooperative Relations,* electronic edition, Department of Sociology, University of Oxford:176-193. http://www.sociology.ox.ac.uk/papers/hart176-193.doc 10 May 2006.

Hearn, A.H. 2006. "Economic Reform in Cuba and China." In

Hernandez-Reguant, A. 2002. "Radio Taíno and the Globalization of the Cuban Culture Industries." Unpublished PhD thesis, University of Chicago.

_____. 2009. "Writing the Special Period: An Introduction." In Hernandez-Reguant, A. (ed.) *Cuba in the Special Period: Culture and Ideology in the 1990s.* New York: Palgrave Macmillan, pp. 1-18.

Hoffmann, B. 2004. *The Politics of the Internet in Third World Development: Challenges in Contrasting Regimes with Case Studies of Costa Rica and Cuba.* New York: Routledge.

Holbraad, M. 2004. "'Religious "Speculation"': The Rise of Ifa Cults and Consumption in Post-Soviet Cuba," *Journal of Latin American Studies* 36: 643-663.

Holgado Fernández, I. 2000. *¡No es fácil! Mujeres cubanas y la crisis revolucionaria.* Barcelona: Icaria Antrazyt.

Horst, H. & Miller, D. 2005. "From Kinship to Link-Up: Cell Phones and Social Networking in Jamaica," *Current Anthropology* Vol 46:755-778.

Howes, D. 1996. "The Mirror of Consumption," in Howes, D. (ed.) *Cross Cultural Consumption: Global Markets Local Realities.* London: Routledge, pp. 1-18.

Humphrey, C. 1995. "Creating a Culture of Disillusionment: Consumption in Moscow, a Chronicle of Changing Times." In Miller, D (ed.) *Worlds Apart: Modernity Through the Prism of the Local.* London and New York: Routledge, pp. 43-68.

Isasi-Diaz, A.M. 2004. *La Lucha Continues: Mujerista Theology.* New York: Orbis.

Kalathil, S. & Boas, T.C. 2003. *Open Networks, Closed Regimes: The Impact of the Internet on Authoritarian Rule.* Washington DC: Carnegie Endowment for International Peace.

Kenedi, J. 1981. *Do-It-Yourself: Hungary's Hidden Economy.* London: Pluto Press.

Kildegaard, A.C. & Orro Fernandez, R. 1999. "Dollarization in Cuba and Implications for the Future Transition," *Cuba in Transition 9:25-35.*

Klak, T. 1994. "Havana and Kingston: Mass Media Images and Empirical Observations of Two Caribbean Cities in Crisis," *Urban Geography* 15:318-344.

Knauer, L.M. 2009. "Audiovisual Remittances and Transnational Subjectivities." In Hernandez-Reguant, A. (ed.) *Cuba in the Special Period: Culture and Ideology in the 1990s.* New York: Palgrave Macmillan, pp. 159-177.

Kopytoff, I. 1998. "The Cultural Biography of Things: Commoditization as Process." In Appadurai, A. (ed.) *The Social Life of Things: Commodities in Cultural Perspective.* Cambridge: Cambridge University Press, pp. 64-94.

La Pastina, A, Rego, C.M. & Straubhaar, J.D. 2003. "The Centrality of Telenovelas in Latin America's Everyday Life: Past Tendencies, Current Knowledge, and Future Research," *Global Media Journal* Vol 2(2), *http://lass.calumet.purdue.edu/cca/gmj/contents.htm.*

Ledeneva, A. 1998. *Russia's Economy of Favours: Blat, Networking and Informal Exchange.* Cambridge: Cambridge University Press.

Lewis, O., Lewis, R.M. & Rigdon, S.M. 1977. *Four Women: Living the Revolution. An Oral History of Contemporary Cuba.* Urbana: University of Illinois Press.

_____. 1978. *Neighbors: Living the Revolution. An Oral History of Contemporary Cuba.* Urbana: University of Illinois Press.

Linkogle, S. 1998. "Soya, Culture and International Food Aid: The Case of a Nicaraguan Communal Kitchen," *Bulletin of Latin American Research* Vol. 17(1): 93 – 104.

Low, S. 1996. "The Anthropology of Cities: Imagining and Theorizing the City," *Annual Review of Anthropology* Vol 25, pp. 383-409.

McCracken, G. 1988. *Culture and Consumption: New Approaches to the Symbolic Character of Consumer Goods and Activities.* Bloomington: Indiana University Press.

Malinowski, B. 1960 [1922]. *Argonauts of the Western Pacific: An Account of Native Enterprise and Adventure in the Archipelagos of Melanesian New Guinea.* London: Routledge & Kegan Paul.

Mandelblatt, B. 2007. "A Transatlantic Commodity: Irish Salt Beef in the French Atlantic World," *History Workshop Journal* 63: 18-47.

Marrero, L. 1983. *Cuba, Economía y Sociedad. Volumen IX: Azúca, Ilustración y Conciencia.* Madrid: Playor.

Marshall, L. 1961. "Sharing, Talking and Giving: Relief of Social Tensions among !Kung Bushmen," *Africa*, Vol 31(3): 231-249.

Mauss, M. 1990 [1954]. *The Gift: The Form and Reason for Exchange in Archaic Societies.* London: Routledge.

Mesher, G.M., Briggs, R.O., Goodman, S.E., Press, L. & Snyder, J.M. 1992. "Cuba, Communism & Computing," *Communications of the ACM* 35:27-29, 112.

Miller, D. 1987. *Material Culture and Mass Consumption.* Oxford: Basil Blackwell.

_____. 1995. "Consumption Studies as the Transformation of Anthropology." In Miller, D. (ed.) *Acknowledging Consumption: A Review of New Studies.* London and New York: Routledge, pp. 264-295.

_____. 2001. "The Poverty of Morality," *Journal of Consumer Culture* 1:225-243.0

_____. 2006. "Beyond Social Science: Social Reproduction in South London." Eighth Annette Weiner Memorial Lecture, New York University Department of Anthropology.

_____. (ed.) 2009. *Anthropology and the Individual.* Oxford: Berg.

Mintz, S.W. 1974. "The Caribbean Region," *Daedalus* 103(2):45-71.

_____ 1986. *Sweetness and Power: The Place of Sugar in Modern History.* New York: Penguin Books.

Mintz, S.W. & DuBois, C. 2002. "The Anthropology of Food and Eating," *Annual Review of Anthropology* 31:99-119.

Mollona, M. 2005. "Factory, Family and Neighborhood: The Political Economy of Informal Labor in Sheffield," *Journal of the Royal Anthropological Institute,* Vol 11(3):527-48.

Molyneux, M. 1996. *State, Gender and Institutional Change in Cuba's 'Special Period': The Federación de Mujeres Cubanas.* London: Institute of Latin American Studies.

Moore, R. 1997 *Nationalizing Blackness: Afrocubanismo and Artistic Revolution in Havana, 1920–1940.* Pittsburgh: University of Pittsburgh Press.

Morris, E. 2008. "Cuba's New Relationship with Foreign Capital: Economic Policy-Making since 1990," *Journal of Latin American Studies* Vol 40(4):769-792.

Newman, K.S. 1988. *Falling from Grace: The Experience of Downward Mobility in the American Middle Class.* London: Collier Macmillan Publishers.

Nickles, S. 2002a. "More is Better: Mass Consumption, Gender and Class Identity in Postwar America," *American Quarterly,* Vol 54 No. 4: 581-622.

_____2002b. "Preserving Women: Refrigerator Design as Social Process in the 1930s," *Technology and Culture* 43(4): 693-727.

O'Dougherty, M. 2002. *Consumption Intensified: The Politics of Middle-Class Daily Life in Brazil.* Durham and London: Duke University Press.

Oldenziel, R. & Zachmann, K. 2009. "Kitchens as Technology and Politics: An Introduction." In R. Oldenziel & K. Zachmann (eds.) *Cold War Kitchen: Americanization, Technology and European Users.* Cambridge and London: MIT Press

Orlove, B.S. 1997. "Meat and Strength: The Moral Economy of a Chilean Food Riot," *Cultural Anthropology* 12(2):234 – 68.

Orlove, B.S. & Bauer, A.J. 1997. "Giving Importance to Imports." In Orlove, B.S. *The Allure of the Foreign: Imported Goods in Postcolonial Latin America.* Ann Arbor: University of Michigan Press.

Padrón, C. 2005. *Franceses en el Suroriente de Cuba.* Havana: Ediciones UNION.

Pahl, J. 1990. "Household Spending, Personal Spending and the Control of Money in Marriage," *Sociology* Vol 24(1): 119-38.

Pearson, R. 1997. "Renegotiating the Reproductive Bargain: Gender Analysis of Economic Transition of Cuba in the 1990s," *Development and Change,* Vol 28: 671-705.

Pérez, L. A., Jr. 1993. "Cuba, c. 1930-1959." In L. Bethell (ed.) *Cuba: A Short History.* Cambridge: Cambridge University Press.

_____. 2006. *Cuba: Between Reform and Revolution,* 3rd ed. Oxford and New York: Oxford University Press.

Pérez-López, J. & Díaz-Briquets, S. 2005. "Remittances to Cuba: A Survey of Methods and Estimates," *Cuba in Transition* 15:396-409.

Pérez-López, J.F.1995. *Cuba's Second Economy: From Behind the Scenes to Center Stage.* New Brunswick, NJ and London: Transaction Publishers.

Pertierra, A.C. 2007. "Battles, Inventions, and Acquisitions: The Struggle for Consumption in Urban Cuba." Unpublished PhD thesis, University College London.

_____ 2008. "En Casa: Women Households in post-Soviet Cuba," *Journal of Latin American Studies* Vol. 40 (4):745-769.

_____ 2009. "Private Pleasures: Watching Videos in post-Soviet Cuba," "Caribbean Media Worlds," *International Journal of Cultural Studies* Vol 12 (2):113-130

_____ 2011. "Sustenance in Special Times: Rice and Beans in post-Soviet Cuba." In R. Wilk & and L. Barbosa (eds.) *Rice and Beans: A Unique Dish in a Hundred Places.* Oxford: Berg.

Pertierra, R., Ugarte, E., Pingol, A., Hernandez, J., & Decanay, N. 2002. *TXT-ING Selves: Cellphones and Philippine Modernity.* Manila: De La Salle University Press.

Pine, F. 2002. "Retreat to the Household? Gendered Domains in Post-socialist Poland." In Hann, C. (ed.) *Post Socialism: Ideals, Ideologies and Practices in Eurasia.* London: Routledge

Porter, A. 2008. "Fleeting Dreams and Flowing Goods: Citizenship and Consumption in Havana, Cuba," *PoLAR: Political and Legal Anthropology Review* 134.

Preston Blier, S. 2006. "Vernacular Architecture." In Tilley, C., Keane, W., Küchler, S., Spyer, P. & Rowlands, M. (eds.) *Handbook of Material Culture.* London: Sage, pp. 230-254.

Reid, S. & Crowley, D. (eds.) 2000. *Style and Socialism: Modernity and Material Culture in post-War Eastern Europe.* Oxford: Berg.

Reid-Henry, S. 2007. "The Contested Spaces Of Cuban Development: Post-Socialism, post-Colonialism and the Geography of Transition, "*Geoforum* 38:445-455.

Ries, N. 1997. *Russian Talk: Culture and Conversation during Perestroika.* Ithaca: Cornell University Press.

Rivero, Y. 2007. "Broadcasting Modernity: Cuban Television, 1950-1953," *Cinema Journal* Vol 46(3):3-25.

Rosenberg Weinreb, A. 2007. *Unsatisfied Citizen-Consumers in Late Socialist Cuba.* Unpublished PhD thesis, University of Pennsylvania.

Rosendahl, M. 1997. *Inside the Revolution: Everyday Life in Socialist Cuba.* Ithaca: Cornell University Press.

Ruíz Miyares, J. 1999. "A Look at Media in Cuba," *Peace Review* 11(1):77-82.

Rundle, M.L.B. 2001. "Tourism, Social Change and *Jineterismo* in Contemporary Cuba," *The Society for Caribbean Studies Annual Conference Papers Vol. 2* http://www.scsonline.freeserve.co.uk/olvol2.html 16 January 2006.

St George, R. 2006. "Home Furnishing and Domestic Interiors," In Tilley, C., Keane, W., Küchler, S., Spyer, P. & Rowlands, M. (eds.) *Handbook of Material Culture.* London: Sage, pp 221-230.

Safa, H.I. 1995. *The Myth of the Male Breadwinner: Women and Industrialization in the Caribbean.* Westview Press.

Sampson, S.L. 1987. "The Second Economy of the Soviet Union and Eastern Europe," *Annals of the American Academy of Political and Social Science* Vol 493: 120-136.

Scheper-Hughes, N. 1993. *Death Without Weeping: The Violence of Everyday Life in Brazil.* Berkeley: University of California Press.

Schor, J., Slater, D., Zukin, S. & Zelizer, V.A. 2010. "Critical and Moral Stances in Consumer Studies," *Journal of Consumer Culture* Vol. 10(2):274-291.

Settle, H. 2007. "On Giving and Getting by in Special Period Cuba: Love, Belief and Survival in the World of the Permanent Crisis." Unpublished PhD thesis, Duke University.

_____. 2008. "'The Coca-Cola of Forgetting': Reflections on Love and Migration in a Post-Castro Age," *Transforming Anthropology* 16(2): 173-5

Shack, W.A. 1997 [1971]. "Hunger, Anxiety, and Ritual: Deprivation and Spirit Possession among the Gurage of Ethiopia." In Counihan, C. & Van Esterik, P. (eds.) *Food and Culture: A Reader.* London and New York: Routledge, pp. 125-38.

Shove, E. 1999. "Constructing Home: A Crossroad of Choices." In Cieraad, I. (ed.) *At Home: An Anthropology of Domestic Space.* Syracuse: Syracuse University Press, pp. 130-142..

_____2003. *Comfort, Cleanliness and Convenience: The Social Organisation of Normality.* Oxford: Berg.

Silva, E.B. 2002. "Time and Emotion in Studies of Household Technologies," *Work, Employment and Society* Vol 16(2):329-40.

Silverstone, R. & Hirsch, E. 1992. "Introduction," In Silverstone, R. & Hirsch, E. (eds), *Consuming Technologies: Media and Information in Domestic Spaces.* London & New York: Routledge, pp. 1-15.

Slater, D. 1997. *Consumer Culture and Modernity.* Cambridge: Polity Press.

Slater, D. & Kwami, J. 2005. "Embedded-ness and Escape: Internet and Mobile Use as Poverty Reduction Strategies in Ghana." Information Society Research Group working paper.

Smith, L.M. & Padula, A. 1996. *Sex and Revolution: Women in Socialist Cuba.* Oxford: Oxford University Press.

Sobo, E.J. "The Sweetness of Fat: Health, Procreation and Sociability in Rural Jamaica." In Counihan, C. & Van Esterik, P. (eds.) *Food and Culture: A Reader.* London and New York: Routledge, pp. 256-71.

Stoller, P. 1996. "Spaces, Places and Fields: The Politics of West African Trading in New York City's Informal Economy," *American Anthropologist* Vol 98(4):776-788.

Sullivan, L. & Hernandez, V. 2000. "Cybercyba.com(munist): Electronic Literacy, Resistance, and Postrevolutionary Cuba." In Hawisher, G.E. & Selfe, C.L. (eds.) *Global Literacies and the World-Wide Web.* London: Routledge.

Trouillot, M-R. 1992, "The Caribbean Region: An Open Frontier in Anthropological Theory," *Annual Review of Anthropology* Vol 12:19-42.

Turner, G. & Tay, J. (eds.) 2009. *Television Studies after TV: Understanding Television in the Post-Broadcast Era.* New York: Routledge.

Vann, E. 2005. "Domesticating Consumer Goods in the Global Economy: Examples from Vietnam and Russia," *Ethnos* Vol 70 (4):465-88.

Varis, T. 1984. "The International Flow of Television Programs," *Journal of Communication* Vol 34(1):143-152.

Verdery, K. 1996. *What Was Socialism, and What Comes Next?* Princeton: Princeton University Press.

Weinreb, A.R. 2007. "Unsatisfied Citizen-Consumers in Late Socialist Cuba." Unpublished PhD thesis, University of Pennsylvania.

Weismantel, M.J. 1988. *Food, Gender and Poverty in the Ecuadorian Andes.* Philadelphia: University of Pennsylvania Press.

Whiteford, M.B. 1974. "Neighbors at a Distance: Life in a Low-Income Colombian Barrio." In Cornelius, W.A. and Trueblood, F.M. (eds.) *Latin American Urban Research Volume 4: Anthropological Perspectives on Latin American Urbanization.* London: Sage Publications, pp. 157-82.

Whitfield, E. 2008. *Cuban Currency: The Dollar and "Special Period" Fiction.* Minneapolis: University of Minnesota Press.

Wilk, R. 2001. "Consuming Morality," *Journal of Consumer Culture* Volume 1(2): 245-60.

_____ . 2006. *Home Cooking in the Global Village: Caribbean Food from Buccaneers to Ecotourists.* Oxford: Berg.

Wilson, M. 2009. "Ideas and Ironies of Food Scarcity and Consumption in the Moral Economy of Tuta, Cuba," *JASO-online* N.S. Vol 1(2):161-178.

World Health Organization. 2010. *World Health Statistics.* Geneva: World Health Organization.

Wirtz, K. 2004. "Santeria in Cuban National Consciousness: A Religious Case of the Doble Moral," *Journal of Latin American Anthropology* 9(2):409-438.

Yurchak, A. 2005. *Everything Was Forever, until It Was No More: The Last Soviet Generation.* Princeton: Princeton University Press.

Index

Order Form

Caribbean Studies Press
7550 NW 47th Ave.
Coconut Creek, FL 33073
Tel: 954-968-7433; Fax:954-970-0330
E-mail: caribbeanstudiespress@earthlink.net.
www.caribbeanstudiespress.com

Name: _____

Address: _____

Telephone: _____

Please send the following:

Quantity	Title	Price	Sub-Total
	Tax(6% for Florida Residents)		
	Shipping 10% of Total (Minimum $4.95)		
	Total:		

Please make Check Payable to Educa Vision Inc.
We accept Visa and MasterCard.

You might also be interested in:

Fieldwork Identities In The Caribbean
Erin B. Taylor.
Softcover. 258pp.
$27.50
ISBN: 978-1-58432-482-9
Cat#: CSP4829

Caribbean Landscapes An Interpretive Atlas
Brothers, Wilson, Dwyer. Softcover.
249 pp.
$59.00
ISBN: 978-1-58432-459-1
Cat#: CSP4591